I Dreamt of a Man

by Bridget Reneé Everson

DORRANCE
PUBLISHING CO
EST. 1920
PITTSBURGH, PENNSYLVANIA 15238

Dorrance Publishing Co
585 Alpha Drive
Pittsburgh, PA 15238
Visit our website at www.dorrancebookstore.com

ISBN: 978-1-6480-4098-6
eISBN: 978-1-6480-4914-9

Content

Acknowledgment . . . .*v*

Introduction . . . .*vii*

I.   *Special Delivery* *1*

II.   *Bullying the Bullies* *7*

III.   *OMG, Is it Over Yet* *13*

IV.   *Love is a Fool's Game* *25*

V.   *Mister Forever* *35*

VI.   *Floridian Crave* *41*

VII.   *What the Enemy Meant for Evil, God Meant It for Good* *47*

VIII. *Gorgeous Was His Name* *55*

IX.   *Death Comes Knocking at My Door* *65*

X.   *There Was a Runaway Train That Came Plowing Through* *69*

XI.   *The Sound of the Mother Land, Africa is A-Calling* *75*

XII.   *The Great Awakening* *91*

Conclusion *95*

A Prayer for You *99*

I Dreamt of a Man *101*

An Apology for My Enemies *103*

Notes *105*

Acknowledgment

I *Dreamt of a Man* came from a whispering in my ear I heard it many years ago. I tried to put it in a script, but that was not God's plan. I put it away, and I heard God say to put it in a book. I was not listening, and he started showing it on television when I sat down to watch a movie with nothing to do with a book; the movie would be about some author, either he or she would be world-renowned as an author or a no one who made it to the top overnight. I cannot begin to thank God enough for him allowing me to accomplish this task; it is astronomical. You see, I had a severe stroke that caused me memory loss; my left carotid artery is completely blocked, meaning that if there is ever too much pressure on that artery I could, well, you know the rest, and I have vertigo, a disease that causes severe dizziness and nausea. With all of this going against me, just look at God. He really wanted me to share with you all my story. God knew that the world needed to hear my story. He poured it back into me like never before; we serve an AWESOME God! He is my Daddy, father, my all and all, Jesus, my friend until the end; he is The Great I Am!

To my daughter, my Superstar, my constant friend, Bre'. She continued push me to tell this story for everyone in the whole world to read. She knew it better than me, that there was something inside of me that had to be released. Every day she applied pressure with the gentlest little voice saying, "What chapter are you on, Mommy? Always saying remember, God gave you a deadline." Never pushing, and for that Mommy LOVES you, Bre', my baby girl.

There is one other person that I cannot forget, Mrs. Bessie Hill. She taught me English at A.H. Parker High School in Birmingham, AL. She was my absolute all-time favorite teacher. Mrs. Hill did not tolerate any tomfoolery in her class, and she loved her students like they were one of her children, and if you cared about learning, she ensured that you were an extraordinary pupil, well read, versed, and you became a skilled member of society. Mrs. Hill showed such strong admiration for those who chose to further their education beyond high school. For one of the world's best teachers, I thank you for everything that you deposited into me to make me the woman that I am today. For I am a strong, educated, and intelligent black woman, and you played such a vital role in my growth process. Mrs. Bessie Hill, thank you, from the bottom of my heart.

And to the rest of my many family members and friends, and even to my enemies, I say thank you, because without you, there would not have been a process to lead me to success. And for my enemies, you kept me on my knees and before God on a daily basis, and I can't thank you enough; what a powerful thing you did for me! For today I am FREE! I am a survivor of Narcissism! Thank God, for everything that he allowed me to go through to achieve my freedom! And I am AWAKE!

Introduction

I *Dreamt of a Man* is full of my real-life events, and there is always an intervention of the Lord. And I want to express my apologies early for the use of some very strong and foul language, as well as picturizations. This type of language helps me to express the feeling in that moment. As it is stated in James 3:8, "But the tongue can no man tame: it is an unruly evil, full of deadly poison." You will see that Satan had me clearly under his control, but when the father has his hands on your life, it seems like you can walk through it without a scar on you, or so I thought. I did that so many times that somehow I began to think that I was invincible and that Satan had no control over my life, but you cannot forget the master, the one who made us all. I forgot about him, even though he was sending people to bring me home to be nearer to him. I ignored them, and I let God slip away from my focus, but instead of him bringing me back, he removed his hands from me, and he let Satan take control of my life. That was the worst thing that could have happened to me. I went through hell and back, but after I had been sick, talked about, left out in the dark, family and friends turned their backs on me and had lost just about everything, I realized that God had not left me, he had let me do things in my own way, but he never left me, and now I have a story that the whole world must know.

I am willing to tell it to you all because I know that there are others like me, that are trying to do it all on their own, but I am here to tell you that you cannot do it without prayer and the leadership and guidance of our Lord. See in the word of God, it says in Proverbs 1:7, "The fear of the Lord is the beginning of knowledge, but fools despise wisdom and instruction."

This is what I should have had, the fear of the Lord, because he was trying to give me wisdom, but there was no fear until situations presented themselves, and I was so afraid that death was going to be my only exit, but I was covered by the prayers of my grandmother and my mother. And if you never hear another word that I am saying to you, prayer really works; it works when you are nowhere near the person that you have prayed for, so if it is your children, grandchildren, a spouse, or even a loved one, continue to be in prayer for them. I promise the Lord always hears you when you call upon him. So, people, this is the moment that I will reveal my inside outward and try to tell you the story of my life, because God said that I have nothing to fear any more. And he gave me this life to be shared with the world. I am sure that a lot of my story is familiar to some of you, and I pray that you all use me as an example and don't repeat my steps taken but take the right way home. It will serve you well and make me immensely happy; it will mean the world to me to see you win. And to God be the GLORY for he gave me a true testimony. Writing this book made me laugh, cry, sing, shout, pray, and wonder what in the world was I going through in my mind; was I crazy or just completely out to save myself and my beloved friends in Christ who are in need of my story?

Some of my thoughts and actions will make you say, "How did she get it done, something like this at this time?" I will completely leave myself exposed for the world, to decide. Why? I have asked myself that too many times, and two answers come to mind.

The first being that I am in a healing process, and God says to tell everyone what you have been through. Second, I know there is a little girl or a woman, or even a man, out there that needs to know that it is okay to have so much hidden baggage. We don't have to be scared; we can come from behind the curtains. The Boogey Man is gone, and it is alright to tell someone that I have been hurt and that the pain from the scars are still there, and I am trying to heal, but they are easily reopened.

I sincerely believe that I can be healed, such as the woman in Luke 8:43-47,

> And a woman was there who had been subject to bleeding
> for twelve years, but no one could heal her. She came up be-

hind him and touched the edge of his cloak, and immediately her bleeding stopped. "Who touched me?" Jesus asked. When they all denied it, Peter said, "Master, the people are crowding and pressing against you." But Jesus said, "Someone touched me, I know that power has gone out from me."Then the woman, seeing that she could not go unnoticed, came trembling and fell at his feet. In the presence of all the people, she told why she had touched him and how she had been instantly healed. Then he said to her, "Daughter, your faith has healed you. Go in peace."

You see, I believe with all that is within me that I am healed and that you, too, will be healed as you read this book. The Lord is going to do some awesome things in your lives, and you will receive a miracle just like the woman in Luke 8. There is absolutely nothing that is impossible for God to do. The only thing that God can't do is fail. There are women who are crying out for help and can't find anyone, but their help is here, and his name is Jesus. I know that you feel as though the evil entity is walking all over you, with those dirty, filthy feet of Satan. But I have a way out, a way for all my friends who have been trying to catch their breath, but now they can breathe again without worrying about if someone or something is going to come and try to suffocate them. Just hold on, because I have been where you are, needing to breathe with no oxygen anywhere, but Jesus is all the air that you will need. Jesus restored my DESTINY! Forever will I praise his name!

God was a light for me, and I know that he can be a light for you all in the darkest hour. Never give up, never give in, because the enemy can and will be beaten by you with all your prayers, and if you don't know how to pray, just call on the name of Jesus; it is sweetest name that I have ever known. Don't you ever stop calling on him, whenever you need him, just call him and begin to tell him, by saying, "Father, I need you every hour of every day; I need you." And by you offering those simple words of prayer, he begins to smile and listen and goes to work on your behalf. You see, God already knows your needs, wants, and desires before you began to ask for anything. As you knock, the door will be open. For as it says in the word, Luke 11:9, "And I say unto you, Ask, and it shall be given you; seek, and ye shall find; knock, and it shall be opened unto you." So, hang on in there no matter how tough things get, no matter how things may look, you have got to hang in there, because our God is not a liar. Numbers 23:19, "God is not a man, that he should lie; neither the son of man, that he should repent; hath he said, and shall he not do it? or hath he spoken, and shall he not make it good?" I have dated many men without the knowledge of the enemy using me. The enemy played me like a puppet on a string, and I did just what he wanted me to do and who he wanted me to do it to. Until I became exhausted with my disgusting lifestyle. No matter how tired you may become keep praying, because God has an answer for you. Do not let Satan steal your joy or destroy your destiny; I am a living, breathing example of how he tried to steal my destiny and destroy what God had placed in me for the world to see and hear. I am excited to tell you all what God did for me, and he surely can and will do it for you.

Chapter I

Special Delivery

My mother was a pretty but a plain, shy girl who had fallen in LOVE with an outgoing and rambunctious young man from the wrong side of the tracks. His family members would always refer to him as BayBro, and folks on the street would call him Jealous Eye. I still sometimes wonder why they called him Jealous Eye. Was it because he had so little growing up, and he was always jealous of things that others had, or was it because he was a very handsome young man, or was it their way of reversing their actual behavior on him? You know how black folks have their crazy ways of doing things. I may never know, but I do know that he did not leave a great impression on my grandmother. She did not like my father one bit, and she told my mother often that she had made a mistake and one day she would see. That day came sooner rather than later.

Well, it came up, and it had to come out that my mother was pregnant with me, Renee'. My mother knew that her mother would be angry, but she had no idea of how my grandmother's temper could over rule her sensibility. My mother decided to tell my grandmother, who was a tall, beautiful, black, half Indian and African American woman, that she was pregnant, and my grandmother slapped my mother's behind down to the floor. My mother, crying out of guiltiness, embarrassment, and shame and my grandmother filled with anger because she knew that her dreams for my mother were all gone, and for what? Some stupid kid from the wrong side of the tracks. And at that very moment, it is my belief that the door was left cracked long enough for Satan to enter in, just through a very small opening is all that it took. It is said in John 10:10 (KJV) that "the thief cometh not, but for to steal, and to kill and to destroy."

So, my mother married the man that my grandmother had the greatest doubts about him becoming anything great. At the same time, my mother was doing the same thing that a woman would have done during that time, because that was what they did in '60s. My mother would always tell me that my father was such a good man in the beginning of their marriage, but he let the streets take him over with drinking alcohol and trashy women. When a woman loves a man, I am thinking that is what was meant when Barbara Ann fell madly, head over heels in love with Leroy. I guess you could say she was an addict for my father's love; she would do anything for him, and she would take almost all his mess. Sounds like a WIFE! The only good thing was that my mother was an exceptional woman. I won't say anything about my daddy that is not true; I will let you decide. Remember, every person in my life was a part of the process. They were meant to do what they did to me.

Daddy

Daddy, you were supposed to be my champion.

Daddy, you were supposed to be my protector.

Daddy, you were supposed to provide for me when no one else would do it.

Daddy, what happen to you?

Daddy, I could not find you.

Daddy, I am not seeing you.

Daddy, is that you over there?

Daddy, who are all those women with you?

Daddy, why can't I stay?

Daddy, why are you sending me away?

Daddy, come with me; you are my champion, aren't you?

Daddy, please come with me; you have to protect me!

Daddy! I AM LOST WITHOUT YOU!

When you would look at my parents, you would think that there is a couple that was made for one another. My mother, a beautiful light-skinned woman that the men just loved, but once they saw him cut the rug with my mom, they just absolutely adored my mommy. That just made my daddy weak, so very weak for my mommy. That is how they started their love, and you could see all the fireworks leading up to me, Miss Quiet and Shy Renee'; I was so NOT quiet.

Now that I know what I know about my Lord and the devil, I do believe that there were angels and demons in that delivery room at Holy Family Hospital. The demons were there because God had placed an anointing on my head, and this anointing disturbed Satan. He could not take it that a child was going to be born on this night that could possibly bring devastation to the kingdom of hell. He was in the room prancing all around, nervously awaiting my arrival.

I was born on October 5th. My mommy was in the delivery room all alone; the nuns had left her. She would tear you out a new rear end with her bare hands, and I know that she would without a doubt, because she was in such great pain and sweating like a negro picking cotton. But back then, she was just content with pushing and getting me out of her. She told me she had a time with delivering me. The nuns that were with her, they left her all alone without any instruction or care; they just told her when she had another contraction, she was to push and that is what my mother did, she bore down and sat up in that empty delivery room with no one there but she and Jesus and Satan. She gave it a push like it was the last thing she was going to do on Earth, and she reached down between her legs, and I came out and cried so loud that the nuns came running into the delivery room. My mother laid back, and the nuns said, "You have a fine baby girl." My mother said the nuns could not take their eyes off me, and she was just wondering what they were looking at, and then one of the sisters spoke, and she told my mom that I was going to be a special person and that God had a placed a special anointing on me. To hear this made Satan furious; he had to stop this from happening. My mother, not caring now, just wanted me in her arms; they let her hold me for a moment, and then they told her they were going to take me to the cathedral for prayer, and they would return me once I was cleaned up. My mommy, feeling so weak, told them okay. My mother does not recall how long they were gone with me, but she remembers them bringing me back. As the sister handed me over to my mother, she said that the sister told her once again that I was a very special child and that she was to take very good care of me. Somehow that excitement about me stopped, I can imagine the devil in hell stood up and said, "THERE WILL NEVER BE ANYTHING SPECIAL OR UNIQUE ABOUT THIS CHILD'S LIFE" AND STOMPED HIS FEET AND YOU COULD HEAR THE CLATTER SOUNDING LIKE THUNDER AS FAR AS THE EARS COULD HEAR! "Oh no, minions, you go right now and check this little brown, infantile thing out and report back to me." The number one man for Satan showed up and was stunned to hear the nuns just going on and on about how wonderful God was and how the whole world would be changed just because of a little girl named Renee'. Satan's minions could not get back to hell fast enough to tell him about me, and Satan became so furious that he stomped and cursed so much that it began to storm, and Satan shouted at his demonic minion, "Destroy her. Leave nothing behind that resembles her! Let there be nothing but misery and pain for as long as she shall live or what most would think would be the end of life as we know it. You got that, God, the Father, the Son, and the Holy Spirit, she is mine!" Him being Satan, burst into laughter, filled with joy, so he thought. But hold on, JUST KEEP WATCH, GOD! As it says in the KJV of the Bible in Psalm 27:1-3, "The Lord is my light and my salvation; whom shall, I fear? The Lord is the strength of my life; of whom shall I be afraid? When the wicked, even mine enemies and my foes, came upon me to eat up my flesh, they stumbled and fell. Though a host should encamp against me, my heart shall not fear though war should rise against me, in this will I be confident." Although I am on the battlefield and Satan is throwing every type of vicious attack at me, I am confident in the God that I serve, and I will not be defeated! For this is what Satan wants of us, to give up and to give in so that he can have victory over another one of God's precious children. So, no matter what you are going through don't give up, and don't ever say I am too tired to continue to run this race. Even as an infant, Satan waged a war against me, because he saw my future and determined that I was going to be a major element in the war that he had begun against our God. So, torture was the name of the game, and this is how it started. The devil set out to destroy my life as he does with all of us. He cannot leave us unattended once he knows that God has something so astronomical for us to do; he will go to any lengths to stop us from succeeding. And in the beginning was where it all started for me. I don't know what made Satan take arms against me, but I do know that once he saw me, he was ANGRY! Can you imagine the devil being that upset with a child? I know that I fell in love with the Lord early, as a little girl, and it turned out that I needed him. My mom said that I loved my father in the beginning, because he gave me so much of his time. And, of course, he loved me. I just wonder what brought about the change in my life's events with my father. That is something that I contemplate occasionally. I think for me it was the first time I saw my father hitting my mother. That was the Jezebel spirit that had taken my father over. A person under the Jezebel spirit does not care about anyone other than himself, a very arrogant personification of a man. My mommy, meaning so much to me, I could not love him in the same way ever again. He would often beat my mother so severely that she would have to be hospitalized. Her face would often be all black and blue. He would change my mother's beautiful face into something horrible to look at, and I do believe that was the devil's aim, to keep my mother down. He tried, but my mother was as strong as a bull; she tried her best to fight. My father was soon to find out that this little girl that could not do anything about him hitting her mother was also a strong being and he and any devil soon would be at war with my God. I was going to soon become one of his worst nightmares. All the people in the community where I lived had respect for the little brown girl with her two ponytails. My destiny now was in my parents' hands, and they knew so little about how to train a child up in the spirit that I was really a lost little lamb, so I thought, but the enemy saw something in me that he could control, because I left the door just cracked wide enough for him to slip right through it. But never, ever stop watching GOD! In Psalm 9:10, it says, "and those who know your name put their trust in you, for you, O Lord, have not forsaken those who seek you." No matter how dark your way becomes, keep praying and always know that our God is forever with you.

Chapter II

Bullying the Bullies

He would beat her just at the thought of another man even glancing at my mom, and her being such a beautiful woman that men would always stop and stare at her. She tried to avoid men, even during social gatherings. It would always end terribly, with my mother trying to get my father off her before he killed her. She was terrified of my father. She told us she was going to stay, because we were her priority; she wanted us to be raised by both of our parents. What a bunch of CRAP! My father was killing us all! And my mother had, once again, put her dreams on hold for her children. This caused me to act out in ways that were unbelievable to other people but that my mother knew that once she heard a siren or a child crying that was when she called my name aloud, "RENEE'". Once I was outside playing with the walkie-talkies that my brother and I had gotten for Christmas, and an idea came to mind. I began to say that a child was stuck in a pipe at Buchannan Construction Company, and I knew that was not the truth, but I continued to call for help; my brother and sister were mortified at my behavior, because they begged me to stop, but I would not. And then came the fire department, paramedics, and ambulance and, let's not forget, the police and my mom! My mother was so angry with me; I can see her face now and hear her voice as she screamed, "Renee', what have you done now?" The police had the guard to open the gates, and they searched every pipe there, and they asked all the people standing around did they know anything about a child being stuck in a pipe, and everyone said no. I got the worst beating of my life, at least that is what I thought of it.

OMGoodness, I must tell you about my experimentation with a magnify glass. I had seen this on the *Electric Company*. I know most of you don't know anything about the *Electric Company* but give me one minute. The experiment was about how a magnifying glass could generate heat from the sun, and placing it on a pile of dry grass, a fire would begin to burn. So, me, I thought I would try it at the Pentecostal Church across the street from where we lived. My little sister Monica went into the house immediately; she said, "I am not getting in trouble with you today." My brother, he wanted to see if it would work, and he stayed until it started to burn. But by it being fall, it burned so quickly my brother was gone in a flash! And I left immediately after I found myself all alone with a fire blazing. Someone must have called the fire department, and here goes my mother's voice once again, "Renee'!" I had almost burned the church down. Once again, I got such a terrible butt swiping, but I won't say it was the worst I had ever gotten, because there were any number of much more painful ones in which I can still feel today. And the worst part about it was that I thought my mommy was a nice and kind woman, but when you did something wrong, it bought out the monster that was lurking down on the inside of her, growling just to come out and have a piece of my little buttocks.

In all my acting out, I wrote my father a letter. He was always angry, and his anger always ended up on my mother's pretty face. I was eleven years old, and my thought process was that of a twenty-year-old. My father was beating my mother on a regular basis, and I couldn't take it anymore. I thought that if I were to write my father, he would feel terrible for the things he was putting my mother through, and us right along with her. The letter was written as follows:

Dear daddy,

Why do you hurt my mother? You say you love her, yet you beat her. You beat her like she is a child of yours, but she has been raised, and her parents never had to beat her, because she was a good girl until the day she met you. You drink all the time, you come home drunk, and you have other women to call our house. You are a bad husband and a terrible father. You need help, because you are also an alcoholic.

Daddy, I no longer love you, and I hope that you will get the help that you need.

> Sincerely your daughter,
> Renee'

The letter was waiting for my father on the coffee table once he got home from work. He read the letter and could not believe that an eleven-year-old girl could have written it. My mother swore she had nothing to do with it, but my father said that she had told me what to write, and he beat her until blood came from her mouth. I tried to help her, but she said no and for me to go to my room. I always felt bad, because I caused her to get a beating that day. So, I never ever wrote another letter to my father again. For me, in that very moment, I did not know what my mother was giving up for me, but I did know that it was a hell of a lot, seeing her beat down with blood flowing from her mouth; I knew it was a lot more than I could ever repay her.

Momma Dreamed Out Loud

Momma, you dreamed so large and so very bright,
who took your dreams away, Mommy?
You dreamed of being successful so that
the world would sing your name out loud!
Momma, who took your baton, and where is your choir?
Momma, you dreamed of a man who could make you smile and never beat
you and never made you cry, why couldn't you find that man, Momma?
What happened to your dreams, Momma?
Are they all gone for good, or are they just deferred?
Dreams are never denied, Momma, just postponed with a momentary delay.
Momma, you are allowed to dream again,
but this time, make them larger than life.

As time grew closer to our moving out from the community, I was growing and changing in every way. I played football with the boys and some of the older girls in our community, and I was the quarterback. I was an okay quarterback; okay, I was a great quarterback. We played full contact, and I was never afraid. I loved football. I even wanted to play when I went to Parker High School. I begged my daddy, but he said, "Are you crazy? There is no way in Hell that you will ever play football, to let all those boys tackle you." Yet, when I was a little girl, I ran over the boys that bullied everyone. They were bigger and really could hurt someone but not me. I would pick up a stick or a mop off of someone's back porch and go to work on their bad asses, and they would stop beating the crap out of all those little kids. I once sent a boy to the hospital, he just wanted to prove that he was the meanest niggar that ever walked at Finley Avenue School, so he chose me to push around, and I was not going to take it, so he shoved me down, and I got up, mad as hell, and I drew back my leg, and I kicked him right in the "BALLS." He fell to the ground, and all the boys who had been cheering for him to beat my ass now left him moaning and groaning in agony. Our coach had seen him shove me down to the ground and nothing was done to me after the coach gave a vivid picture to our principal. And can't you see the devil walking away with his tail between his legs, thinking to himself, "What do I have to do to get rid of this little girl?" But they had to call an ambulance for him. Once he returned to school, all the bullying stopped, and he never said another word to me. So, once I heard my brother singing out my name, "Renee'." I could just imagine those mean boys trying to punish my little brother; he was a cute, chocolate kid with a sweet disposition, and they were not about to ruin that in my brother. My sister Monica and I knew that my brother had done something to someone, but I had to go and get ready for war for my younger sibling. I told Monica to go home, and I was going back to the school to help Bro. I ran all the way back to the school, but when I got there, my brother was picking up his books and walking towards me. I said, "Bro, what happened?" My brother said, "Once those boys heard me calling your name, they all said, 'Oh, no, we are not going to fool with that crazy-ass girl Renee'; she will kick a nigga's ass.'" Bro said, "Then they all left me here alone." What? Those tired-ass boys. That was good that they did, because I came ready to beat their sorry butts. My brother and I laughed, and he said, "I believe that they knew you would be ready to kick their asses!" "That's right, because you are my little brother." We left 14th Street shortly after that and life started to get rougher for us. I had been taken away from my Grandma Edith, she was my security blanket, and when I was in her arms, it seemed like nothing in the world could ever do me any harm. Now, my entire family was living in Thomas.

My daddy was home at last; everybody knew him, and he knew everyone. Have you ever had a dream and woke up and you were living it, it was like déjà vu? It was as though I had already lived in this place. All I could say was Lord help us.

Chapter III
OMG, Is it Over Yet?

Mama

Grandma for most of my life was called Mama
Mama was beautiful, tall, thin and subtle spoken woman
with hair that hung down her back
She was my feel better baby when I was sick
Mama was wiping your face, sugar, when I had cried all night long
When everyone said, "You are so ugly," Mama would say,
"those Niggas don't know you, God made you and you are BEAUTIFUL"
My Mama was Wisdom, and Wonderful and
an Absolutely Awesome Soul, all wrapped up into One!

Now, I must explain my use of Nigga so often; it is not intended as an insult by any means. My grandma gave the best definition of the word Niggar, a niggar was derived from Negro; it was anyone who brought trouble to a situation, be it a white, yellow, or a black man. She said it was in the Webster's dictionary, but I looked it up, and that was not the definition. But I had sworn by this definition of a nigga for my whole life through. There are just some things that you hold on to and you can't release them, because if you do, the world in which we live in it won't make any sense anymore. Like my grandmother, I called anyone a nigga, no matter what the color their skin was. If they did something I considered wrong, then they were niggas. My grandma could make me laugh so much using the word nigga. There were these young white boys that worked at the R. J. Reid Construction Company in which my grandparents lived on the property. These kids always walked over my grandma's front yard. Grandma put so much work into the beautification of her lawn in the middle of a construction company, so when those white boys ignored her sign of, "DO NOT WALK ON THE GRASS," she began to call them niggas, because they were on her well-manicured lawn. And she had told them about walking there once, and now there was a sign, and they were acting as if they could not read. And it was as the definition she had given me, anyone who brings trouble to a situation, regardless of his color, is a nigga. Those white boys laughed at my grandma; they thought that she was crazy, but they got off the grass, and she never had a problem with them again. I knew that leaving my grandma was going to be hard, but I never knew it would be horrible. I could see that ol' devil rejoicing, for he knew he was taking me from my comfort zone, away from my grandma and away from our church, Mount Zion Community Church. The devil made the beast in my father really show out and made him behave like a crazy man filled with jealousy over my mother. The devil could not win, but it was a battle, and it was on!

All I had ever heard was the grass was greener on the other side of town. I just knew things were going to be better, even though we were moving into a neighborhood that was predominately white in 1977, but I just believed that people were different. I had my first opportunity to be in a classroom with white kids at Gorgas Elementary School. I made things hard on myself by being one of the smartest kids in the building. I still did not get along with any of the boys, but there was one white boy that I could not stand. He made the black kids' lives a living hell. He constantly called us niggas and would not let us have any peace without constant harassment. It was awful, but he had never said anything to me directly until the day I was going to band class and he called me a nigga. I turned around, and I was at the bottom of the stairs, and I don't know what happened; it was like something snapped inside of my brain. It appeared he was saying, "Nigga, nigga, nigga," and before I knew it, I was back up those stairs chasing him. He tried to run for the door, but back then, I was much too quick, and my teacher locked the door as though she knew he was going to try and enter. He snatched for the door, and she turned and walked away, and he was stopped. When that door shut after the bell had rung, I knew that I had to give him what he had been asking for his entire life. I beat the living crap out of that white boy and made him promise not to ever call another black person a nigga for as long as he lived, and I made him scream it out loud, "I WILL NOT CALL ANOTHER BLACK PERSON NIGGA AGAIN!" It was not to be a vicious little girl attacking a white boy, but my attack was just so he could hear himself saying those vile and filthy words coming across the lips of a boy, that had never been harmed or hurt by one single black person. When I let him up, he had tears all over his face, and he was all black and blue, and both of his eyes had been blackened. He ran away from the school, and I did not follow up with him to inquire about where he was going. I DIDN'T CARE! One thing that I did know was he was out of my hair and everybody else's who was black.

That evening my father was drinking beer at the corner store, he and some of the white guys he had grown up with sharing a laugh or two, because my father was a Caddy Master at the Vestavia Country Club, and he could make tears fall from your eyes in laughter. But in the middle of their quite humorous conversation comes in my once enemy that I had dethroned that very day. My father said that he knew right there that all hell was about to break out, so he took a big gulp of his beer, and he waited for the devastating news to erupt. As the boy's father began to question his son, "What the fuck happened to you?" And his son's reply was, "A group of boys got me from behind, and they beat me." "What are you talking about? They beat you from behind and you never saw any of them? Your face looks like you were beaten with a bat." At that point my father told them he would see them later. Once he arrived home, he called me, "Renee'!" My heart was beating, and I was so afraid that I came into the room with my head down. My father said, "What did you do?" And I said, "Daddy, I did not do…" and he stopped me in the middle of a lie. He said, "I saw the damage that you left behind. What could he have done to make you that angry that you would beat him like a Mack truck hit him? What happened?" I told my father that I was called a nigga by the white boy that everyone hated but was afraid to deal with. My father said, "So, you dealt with him and beat the shit out of him." And I said yes in a very low voice as I looked up at my daddy. My brother and sister were standing back, watching and hoping that I wouldn't get a beating for what I did. My father said, "Renee', you know you can't beat up everyone for calling you a nigga, huh?" I said yes, but in the back of my head I was saying, "What about giving them a severe ass swiping?" Then my father went on to tell me that the white boy's family were all probably members of the KKK, and they would not rest until they knew the truth. My father said, "Do you understand where that places me?" And at that point, I knew that my father was afraid but that he loved me enough that he was going to do whatever he had to do to protect me. He told all of us that the people who had dumped trash on our yard were nothing in comparison to the people that could come in retaliation for my acts of revenge against that white boy. My father sent me to my room to think about what I had done, but as I turned and looked back at my father, he had a smile on his face as he was shaking his head and looked at me and nodded, saying it is going to be okay. As we waited with bated breath, nothing ever happened; the Klan did not come for us, and I thought I slipped through again. And that white boy's slow process of healing must have given him a chance to think about what he had done, and the torture stopped, and before we knew it, he had graduated and was off to start fires somewhere else. But as for me, that was not the end of my time as a rebel but only the beginning.

During that summer we went to summer camp at Camp Fire West. It was a nice camp, and we were lucky to be there. But just as Satan does, there were two girls there that just hated me. The black girl must have been in high school, but one thing was for sure, she hated the mere sight of me, and I can't imagine why there was so much animosity between the two of us. After so many days of seeing me, she had devised a plan to kill me, and it nearly worked. There must have been someone praying for me. Isaiah 54:17: "No weapon formed against me shall prosper; and every tongue that shall rise against thee in judgement thou shalt condemn." This person that the enemy had taken control of, like a puppeteer, had decided that there would be no more Renee' for her to have to look at after swim class. So, as the swim class began, she found her way over to me and sat her body on top of me, holding my head under the water, and by there being so many kids in the pool, the lifeguard didn't see her holding me down. I struggled and came up for air, coughing and grasping for every breath. While the lifeguard ran over to me, she and her friend, evil demons of Satan, laughed at me. Until this day, I do not swim. Once I got home and told my cousins, it was on! They said, "You will beat her ass," and they taught me how to fight someone of her size, and the next day, it was on! My cousins came the next day, and they found a pit in the back of the camp site, and they told me that it was going down inside of that pit. They had one of their handsome guy friends to trick the girl to come back to the pit, and that was where I was waiting. They told us that it ended today, and they lowered us down into the pit. I knew that I had to win, or all my male cousins would never let me live it down. She hit me first, but after that, I must have lost my mind, and I beat her down. All that I could hear was my cousins screaming, "Beat her ass. Renee'! She tried to kill you; don't let her get away!" After they got us out of the pit that was the last time that I saw her around the camp. I think that they made me more dangerous and do you know something? I liked it! What I did not know was that me being mean and cruel to that girl was just what the devil wanted from me, and I gave it to him with no resistance. I could see him with my cousins just laughing, not with them but at them; we all got played.

There was a little white girl at the camp with the biggest mouth, and she loved calling me a nigga. I tried not to hit that little girl, but on this day, she must have lost her mind. She stood on a picnic table at the top of the hill, and she called me an ugly, black-ass, stupid nigga. I grabbed her before I knew it and drug her to the ground and beat her so badly that she was taken away in an ambulance. My mom was called, and she came from work, and the camp director put me and my sister out of the camp, and she told my mom that I could have been arrested, but because the girl started it and everyone saw it that was why I wasn't in jail. She told my mom that if she wanted to keep me, she should get control over my temper. My mom just told me and Monica to get into the car. When she got into the car, she broke down and cried, saying that she had done everything possible to keep me out of trouble, but nothing was working. She told me once they came for me there would be no argument, she was going to just let me go. I tried to tell her that I was sorry, but she just wiped her tears and told me that it was okay. I was young, but I knew in my heart that it was not okay.

My mother had so many rules for her children to follow and breaking one rule back in the day where all the adults in the neighborhood were your momma and daddy meant trouble. They would tell you that they were going to tell on you and you best believe if they said it, it was done. My mother had this one rule for us all and that was no company until she came home from work. But I was so in love with my neighbor, I just had to have him over. We were laughing and talking until my sister came out and all his attention shifted from me to her. Then it was all about Monica, so I left and went inside, but I told Monica it was getting close to time for Momma to come home, but Monica thought that because the guy came to see me that she would be okay. As soon as my mother turned the corner at the Catholic church, she saw Monica sitting on the steps with a boy and that was all that she needed to lose her mind. She sent my neighbor home and called Monica inside immediately. Monica told her that the boy was there visiting me, but my mother said, "Then where was Reneé'?" I was angry with Monica for taking my company, so I let my mother beat my sister uninterrupted. I felt justified; however, my sister felt betrayed and harbored a grudge for many years. My sister had shared this story with her children and her friends, but never said a word to me. When her baby brought it to my attention, I laughed but my sister was still angry, so I apologized, and she still said, "I don't accept your apology, because you were wrong." That is where I left it, because life is too short to be concerned over something from over thirty years ago. And my sister could never hold anything against me, because she knows she means the world to me and that was what we all were taught. But the door was left cracked open, and the devil stuck his foot in and made my sister so angry with me; she has not been the same with me since, and the devil wins the battle with something as small as a toenail.

While I was at A. H. Parker High School, I just wanted it to be over. I was tired of being called ugly by everyone that seemed to be somebody. And my father was just adding to it with all the beatings that he was giving my mother; it was a nightmare. One night my father had beat my mom so bad while we were out that the neighbors had called the police and an ambulance. When I came up to the porch my father was sitting there drunk, smoking a cigarette, and they had tried to get my mother to press charges, but she was being indecisive out of fear, I am sure. So, my father, who I know now was acting out of the devil's handy work, turned to me and began to lash out at me. He told me, in front of the policemen, that no one would ever want me except for my sex. He took another puff off the cigarette and blew it up into the air and said to me that I was nothing and would never be nothing. As tears rolled down my face, he sat there laughing aloud. For only if I were a stronger person back then, I would have known that my father was not speaking on his own. As it is stated in Matthew 16:23, "Jesus turned and said to Peter, 'Get behind me, Satan! You are a stumbling block to me, you do not have in mind the concerns of God, but merely human concerns.'" The police officer was infuriated with my father, and he said, "Why did you say such horrible things to your daughter? She is your flesh and blood. You need to take them back," and my father just laughed and laughed. The policeman left us standing there, and he said, "I am so sorry that your father said that to you; if there is anything that we can do please, do not hesitate to call us."

As my time drew near, and my graduation came closer, I was so excited about the schools in which I had applied to, because it meant that I would be leaving the constant criticism and harassment of my peers and family members. The never-ending name calling of "big nose," "big lips," and "ugly." I was leaving Parker as salutatorian, known for being smart with a beautiful body but an ugly face. One day I was in class before everyone, my face wet with tears, I had been talked about all the way into class. Before I knew it, there was a boy that I really liked; he came in and saw me trying to hide my tears, and he stopped to touch my face, and he said, "Why are you crying?" I told him that everyone hated me and talked about me and called me names. He said, "You are beautiful; they are just too blind to see who you really are. I know that you are hurting, but you will grow into every one of your unique features, and you will be the best looking one of all the girls. Watch and see," is what he whispered into my ear as the rest of the class came pouring into the room. He sat in the desk behind me and smiled as I took a quick glimpse of him to say quietly, "Thank you."

My mother was very proud and excited for me, but she did not want me to go far from her. My father was proud of me in his own way, but his talk with me about my major was so disheartening. I wanted to be a black Barbara Walters. I wanted to be a top news journalist and anchor on the evening news. When I told my father about my plans, he burst out into laughter and said, "You are much to dark, and no one would want to look at you; you are not attractive." The tears rolled down my face, and he acted as if he did not see me crying and just told me that I should be a doctor or a nurse, because it does not matter how you look when you are saving someone's life. I got up and went to my room and no one came to console me; it was if they all agreed. I cried myself to sleep. When I woke up, I had a plan, a plan to end all the ungodly terrible things I had been going through. It was going to end that day after I came home from school. I was going to get the biggest knife we had and end it all. That day, I came home, I dropped my books, and went into the kitchen and found the largest knife I could and went into the bathroom with tears in my eyes and looked into the mirror, and as I began telling myself that I was too ugly and too black to live, there was a soft and gentle voice that came across as clear as day, and it was saying, "Why do you want to do this Renee'?" I looked around, and the voice said, "Don't you know that I love you?" At that point, I said, "Who is this?" Then I heard the voice say, "Don't do this because there is so much that you must do, please. 'Satan comes to steal, kill and devour.'" John 10:10. At that very moment I knew that Satan had tried to convince me to take my life, but my savior, Jesus, had intervened and saved me once again. It was not the first and it would not be the last time. I began to cry and cry as I went into the kitchen. All that I could hear and see was me standing in the bathroom mirror with the knife in hand and the enemy speaking fast slick conversation, as he sat on my left shoulder whispering, "Go ahead; no one will care. They showed you already that don't care about you, and they will be better off without you." Jesus sitting on my right shoulder saying, "But why are you doing this, my child? Don't you know how precious you are to me? I love you. Don't do this, because I have so much for you to do. Please, take the knife back and put it away." Jesus won this battle, and the devil went back to hell with his hung down.

In my home was where the guys from my brother's football team spent time hanging out, and even some of the troublesome kids. There were never any problems in my home. I guess you could say we had one of the cool moms in the community. My mom fed these guys and my brother, and I loved my mom for all she did to help us fit in to a place where we did not belong. I was always aware that I had a brother and a sister coming up behind me, so I had to maintain my reputation of being a good girl, coming from a respectful home, no matter what was going on behind closed doors. My brother even came to us, telling us how he had been in the locker room at school and heard some of the guys talking about how fine I was, but I was not giving it up to anyone. He told my daddy he was proud to be my brother. My father just agreed.

As I was on my countdown now to graduating; I had fallen in love with the very handsome guy who delivered the newspapers. He was such a sweet guy to me, and I felt that I had to please him. He made me feel loved and that was a part of my sadness; I felt like I needed a daddy figure, and this was my way of having a lover and daddy all wrapped up into one. We had talked about becoming sexually active, but I felt like it was too soon. I didn't want to lose him so, I invited him over one day after I got out of school early. Once he arrived, I had on my panties and bra, and I let him see what he could have, and I slowly let his hands run over every curve of my body, and I kissed him as I sat in his lap and as he was growing inside of his pants and I knew from all that I had heard and seen on television that it was enough teasing my sweet, sexy boyfriend. I told him that I would be ready soon, and he grabbed me and pulled me close and planted his lips up against mine, and for a moment, I could not feel my legs as he made me promise that he would be the first man that I would make love to. I promised him, because he made my heart skip a beat every time I saw him, always smiled when he saw me, and he placed first as the love of my life!

The day I had been waiting on was finally here, graduation day. I was so very excited; I could hardly breathe. I was to speak as salutatorian, and that made me nervous. As I was preparing for my big day, I thought of all the laughter, tears, and pain. I remembered, as I was sitting in front of the mirror, how many times Monica and I had practiced for choir, because we sung in Mount Zion Community Church Youth Choir and how we would laugh at ourselves for everything. I even remembered those rainy Sunday evenings when I would take a nap and how I loved the smell of the rain coming through the open windows as the breeze blew back the curtains; I could see myself inhaling the cool fresh breeze. I could see myself lying in bed for hours talking with my one and only boyfriend, how wonderful! I, however, could remember all the terrible times I had that made me cry and made me hate Birmingham and made me want to run, not walk, away from the city where, unknown to me, the ugly duckling, was becoming a beautiful swan. I was so ready to leave Alabama; my speech that I delivered as one of Parker High's salutatorians was, to a small degree, saying goodbye to the state of Alabama, and I could not remember anything else after my delivery, except preparing to leave and forgetting all my hurts and past worries.

By the end of the summer, I was so ready to go to Dillard University in New Orleans; I could not hide my excitement. My boyfriend, Marshall, and I had grown so close; we talked every day. We had decided to be with each other before I left for school. The Saturday we planned to be together it stormed and that made it even better, because we both loved the rain. He came and picked me up in the rain, and I felt the cold raindrops hitting me on my face, and I did not care. Marshall made me feel like I was the only woman in the world that mattered. He knew how to make me feel exceptional. When we got to his home, he took me downstairs where we could be alone, and as the rain poured down, he and I became one. It felt like there was no one else on the planet but he and I. I so adored Marshall. That was the day my handsome boy-friend, Marshall, asked me to be his wife and I said, "Of course, I will." He begged me not to go off to school in New Orleans, but I just knew we would be okay; little did I know. When I came home, I could not stop smiling. My sister, Monica, told me I better go and lie down before my mom and dad saw me and knew that I had sex. I was so shocked that she knew, she said, "Girl, anyone could tell you have had sex with that goofy smile on your face." She and I laughed all night. I remember, late that night, Marshall standing outside my window saying he loved me and me returning it with "I love you too," and my father saying, "Boy, if you do not leave from my window, I am going to kill you." That very next morning, we left for New Orleans, and my life would be changed forever and not for the better. I cried as we drove off, because I was leaving Marshall, and I knew he would miss me, because I would surely miss him. In all of your life, have you ever really loved someone so much that you placed them and their needs above those of your own? How has that worked out for you? I did not think that Marshall would not try to stay true to me. I never, ever thought there could be someone else, because Marshall was too kind to me; he never had raised his voice at me. I loved this man with all that was in me. And I just knew that he loved me. Satan was at work; even in my first real relationship, there was deceit and manipulation, as it says in 2 Timothy:1- 5,

> This know also, that in the last days perilous times shall come. For men shall be lovers of their own selves, covetous, boasters, proud, blasphemers, disobedient to parents, un-thankful, unholy, Without natural affection, trucebreakers, false accusers, incontinent, fierce, despisers of those that are

good, Traitors, heady, high minded, lovers of pleasures more than lovers of God; Having a form of godliness, but denying the power thereof: from such turn away.

Chapter IV

Loves a Fool's Game

We all were extremely excited, because we had never been anywhere like New Orleans in our lives. My family was the typical road trip sort of family with one exception, my father. My father was a comedian and, sometimes, an awful drunk. For this trip, he was just a comedian and hilarious. He told us jokes, and my mother had been appointed the designated driver due to a large body of water that had been seen on the diagram of the map to New Orleans. My father smoked like a train, but in between puffs, he said some of the funniest things, and we laughed and laughed as he told one amusing story after another. We had so much fun on the trip that it made my childhood memories seem almost normal, but you and I know that they were not. When we came to Lake Pontchartrain, all the laughter ceased. My father stopped smoking, and I do believe he held his breath until we crossed over that large body of water. You could see that hateful, mean man who tortured his family into submission and had us terrified of him in our own home become a crippled little scared boy. The water was the calming force that my mother needed, it caused my father to relax and to chill completely out. My mother never even saw the little boy that my father became sitting right next to her. Life could have been so much better over time if they could have taken weekends away to the beach, and as my father would have grown accustomed to the water, my mother would have gotten all the credit for her introducing him to the wonderful and tropical experience that only beach life could provide.

We arrived, and New Orleans was as beautiful as I had imagined. The streets were crowded with the most exotic people, and when they spoke, it seemed like a different language. I was so excited to be on campus; I was a real Blue Devil. When I stepped out into the aisle of oaks, I knew that I had made it to a space in time where I would be educated in more ways than one. My family was unloading all of my things and talking to everyone that they met; it was a enlightening but a sad day. My father pulled me to the side, and I thought he was going to say something sweet to me; I must have been on crack. He said, "You know that twelve hundred dollars that your momma made me give you? I want my gotdamn money back; you hear me girl?" I just looked at him, as the tears welled up in my eyes, and I stormed away from him. When it was time to say goodbye to my mother, I could not stop the tears from falling. I felt so bad, like I was leaving her behind. She looked at me and said, "Just remember what I said." She had told me to do my very best, and she knew that I would do well. I promised her that I would do my best. At that moment, I knew that I would always love my mother. When they got into the car, and the tears begin to roll down my face as I waved good bye to them. I felt like I had lost my best friend as they drove out of sight. Deuteronomy 31:6, "Be strong and of a good courage, fear not, nor be afraid of them: for the LORD thy God, he goes with thee; he will not fail thee, nor forsake thee."

The classes had begun, and I had some serious dilemmas with what my father had said to me; "You are unattractive" and "No one wants to see you on television" rang over and over in my head. And so, it was my decision to go into nursing and leave journalism behind. Because who would ever want to see me on television? And that made me cry some more, and besides all of that, I was missing my boyfriend like crazy. I didn't know what to do with myself. I even called my mother to ask if I could go to a party, my mother laughed and said, "You are a young woman, and I trust you to make the right decisions for yourself." What my mother did was release me to be free. I cried for a minute longer, and then something happened. One night I was in the dorm hallway just talking with some girls, and I was about to go to my room when I heard someone say, "Hey." I turned around, and there was the most handsome man I had ever seen. He spoke to me again. I was shocked that he said anything to me, because I had been told that I was so ugly. He spoke to me and said, "Hi, what is your name?" And I replied, "Renee'." "What a beautiful name for such a pretty girl." I asked, "Do you go to school here?" And he said no. He told me he played football for Tulane University. I wanted to know what he came on to Dillard's campus for and he said to meet me. Oh, he had me. I blushed, and he said, "Can I get your number?" and, of course, I gave it to him. He had to leave, because we had a curfew, and that was something that they did not bend the rules on at DU. As he got up to leave, he said, "I will talk to you later, sunshine." I was thinking, why had he called me that? But, as I walked into the restroom and looked into the mirror, it was obvious to me; I was wearing a bright yellow outfit and a gleaming smile that I had been told could light up any room, and I had not seen it in a while. But tonight was a different story. This country girl was smitten by a guy whom I had forgotten to ask him his name. But somehow, news travels quickly when a country girl is talking to a star football player. I found out from one of the girls that his name was Kelvin, and he was a star player for Tulane University. The girls told me that he only came to DU to meet the freshman before the rest of the guys came back to school, but I thought nothing of it, because I had a boyfriend. But then, he called me two days later. He was so nice to me, and I had not been hearing from my boyfriend on a regular basis. Something was going on, but I was so busy trying to keep up with my classes, I did not have the time to dedicate to the thoughts of a boyfriend. I just knew that he was at home missing me as much as I was missing him. But there came a call from someone whom I called a friend, but I knew that she made that one call just to be spiteful, because she always wanted to be with my boyfriend. And she never called me again throughout my entire time in college. So, be very careful whom you call your friend. But I digress. She told me that the man I was saying that I was going to marry had proposed to someone else, and that they were planning their wedding. I was so hurt and distorted over what I heard that I called Marshall, and he told me that his mother had talked with him and told him that I was too dark, and we would have dark skin children, and that was unacceptable in their family. He said he had found someone that was more suitable for him. I asked him, "How could you listen to your mother?" He said, "She is my mother." You know what? Ignorance is truly bliss, and I slammed the phone down in his face. I cried all night until I fell asleep. When I woke up, I felt much better, because I was free. I could move on, and I had someone to move on with, and he was fine as a tall glass red wine, yes! I was going to be okay.

Even though I said I could handle it, school was so difficult, and I was having such a hard time dealing with it all. I missed my mommy, and I wanted to just go home. My birthday came, and to my surprise, all the girls from Alabama paid for me to receive the biggest bouquet of balloons I had ever seen or had. It was such a huge surprise, and they did it all, because I wanted to leave. They wanted me to stay in school to finish what I started. I really appreciated them all. They made me smile and laugh all day, one of the best days with friends. Things were starting to turn around and with very little effort on my part. I was walking to my dorm in the usual way with my head down as I always did, because I had been told I was ugly so often, I did not want anyone to be subjected to looking at me. But this day, an Omega man stopped me and asked why did I walk with my head down all the time. I told him that I was not much to look at and he said, "You are wrong. You are pretty, but if you continue to walk with your head down, no one can see your beautiful face." I looked at him and smiled. He touched my face and said, "Head up," and left. From that moment on, I walked with my head up, proudly displaying the beauty that I had been told to hide from everyone's vison for years. My life had begun to turn around, and I was the happier for it.

Kelvin and I had been talking over the phone, and he had come on campus to visit me a couple of times, but he wanted me to come over to visit him at his place. I was becoming addicted to Kelvin; he was like a drug that I could not go without a single day. I did not want to chance it, but I could not resist a moment of being in the presence of him. He said things to me that no one had ever said to me before. We liked ballet and traveling all over the world. I told him how I loved boxing and football, and he promised me that he would take me everywhere. I could not and would not pass up a night out with this man. When Kelvin arrived, I was so thrilled to see him. He had the most beautiful smile, and he always complimented me on the way in which I dressed. He said I was such a classy country girl, and that made me laugh, because I was working overtime to lose my Southern drawl. He thought the way in which I spoke was so cute, and he loved my body, with all those voluptuous curves. I was his biggest fan, on and off the field. I simply adored Kelvin, and everyone around me knew it; there was no denying it. He made my heart sing.

Just at the mere sight of him, my heart would skip a beat, and it was not just me, he acted as though I was the only woman on the planet, or so he led me to believe that this was true. He opened the door for me in his powder-blue Bug; little did I know then, there would be many trips to follow in this ancient piece of crap that Kelvin worshipped. As I was seated, he reached over to give me a kiss, and there was a huge explosion in my head of stars bursting and soaring all over the midnight skies in my mind, because no one had ever kissed this little country girl like that. As we drove away, I looked at the streets of New Orleans, and not only did I fall in love with Kelvin, but I was also in love with the Cajun, soul-filled sounds and smells of the people and places of New Orleans. For the first time, I realized that I was free; no more daddy to ruin everything. Now Satan had to plan another attack mode, but little did I know, Satan is always around planning ahead.

We entered Kelvin's apartment in which he shared with two other guys. He had a cat that came out from nowhere; she could smell her master was home, but I was dreadfully afraid of cats. Kelvin saw how intimidated I was by his gorgeous white furball and immediately put her away. We sat on his bed, and he offered me something to drink, but I was too nervous. He reached over and began to kiss me and there go the fireworks again. But this time I let him have total control of my body, and he made love to me, and I felt the whole entire world moving; it was damn wonderful! But hold on, wait a minute, let me put some stank in it, screech! Here comes bruh Satan; he can't let a little sister have a meaningful evening with this tall, gorgeous, piece of black, chocolate love, oh, but no! Kelvin wants to continue lying down, but I tell him that I have curfew, as if he did not know, and guess what happens next. He gets up and pulls on his pants and said, "That's what I get for fucking a baby!" He said, "You afraid of being little late for curfew, so bring your butt on, and I will drop you off." I am literally so hurt that tears start to fall down my face. How could someone who just had been so passionate with me, behaving like Doctor Jekyll and Mr. Hyde? As we got close to campus, he said, "I will see you later, and stop that crying; you are making me sick." I guess Satan flipped his lid, stood, and took a bow for the most animated creature that he had ever created. Bravo! Bravo, Satan! As he spread his broad black wings and laughed aloud, it seemed like the earth shook. He had won, and I was down! How lousy I felt and for what? I felt like the pit of the Earth. When

I came into my room, my roommate said, Oh, you are back early." I said, "What are you talking about?" She said, "At twelve, midnight, you set your clock back one hour; you had an extra hour out. OMG! That did not help; that just made me feel worse, and I got into bed fully dressed and cried myself to sleep, because I knew that Kelvin knew the truth about the situation, and once again, I had been played.

For a few days following that huge faux pas. I walked around feeling terrible with nothing on my mind but studying and being the best student that I could be. One day I was sitting outside in the bright and beautiful sunlight, after dining in cafeteria, when someone came up from behind and touched me from behind and asked if he could sit there, and without turning around, I said sure. He touched me again, and said, "What's a beautiful girl like you doing sitting here all alone?" I thought to myself that he was going to be a pain, but when I turned around and saw how gorgeous this tall, black, Creole specimen was, all I could manage to say was hello. Hello was his response to me. He asked me if I had ever had giant shrimp, and I said to him that I had never had shrimp, but what I meant was, I had never eaten any seafood other than fish. I was too ashamed to admit that, because here I was, in a city like New Orleans, and this little old country girl had only eaten fish on Friday. So, him not knowing any better, he told me, "Great, we were going out on Friday." I thought about it and said, "What if the devil is playing another dirty trick on me? What if he is sitting down in hell saying, 'How stupid is this dumb chick?'" and he began to laugh and laugh at me, but this could not be true. The enemy was not concerned about me. I was going out on a date with a handsome guy that appeared genuine.

My mother would always buy me the nicest outfits; she must have saved money for them, because I know some of them could set her back a pretty penny. The first night that Larry took me out, we rode the bus to the French Quarters, and I looked like a million dollars. My hair was so fly, and I had on a beige, wrinkle denim pant suit. Larry could not wait to hold my hand. We laughed and talked about everything, and we ate at his uncle's restaurant, and we drank daiquiris and had a ball. When we left the restaurant, we were walking down Canal Street and laughing and laughing, and I could not stop laughing, because Larry was such a comedian. All the sudden, it got pitch black dark, and I felt myself becoming so afraid, and I was justified; there were cats all around me. I was in a catatonic stupor. I could not walk or speak; I was frozen. I do not know what happened. I just remember Larry shaking me and saying, "Are you alright?", and I answered yes. I told him that I was terrified of cats. He told me we were passing a fish market and cats were all around, and I just stood there like a statue, unresponsive to him, and he just picked me up and walked with me. I was so ashamed that all I could say was I am so sorry. He said that there was not a problem, and he looked at me with those big beautiful eyes, and I knew that he was telling me the truth. Satan was working overtime at this point. He was having private party with me as the guest of honor. I could just see him using Larry, because he was so weak and had no religious base at all. He told me that he was Catholic but the way he got me hooked on "weed," well I begged the difference. Larry's mother was ill, and he had to provide her with care. I could sometimes see it in his face how tired he was of just being there with her. And Satan came right in through that open door, because Larry had left the door open, and that is how Satan plays on our mind; he was able to subdue me and Larry at the same time. So, Satan had another opportunity to take control of me. Can't you just see him, partying, saying "Hey, ho, I got them both," and he was just balling! Larry and I were just partying, going back to his place smoking until we were so high it appeared we were above the clouds looking down onto earth. We even once made love, and I was so high that I came to and Larry was passed out on the bed lying across me, and we were both naked, and his friend had come through the back door and stood there in a drunken stupor, just laughing. That was it for me, so I thought. I was ashamed, and I should have kept this part of my life a secret and to myself, but I thought about it; how could I help people if I was not going to be open and honest about who I really had been in my past? There are people out there hurting today just like I was some thirty years ago, and God said, "Don't be ashamed; that is no longer who you are. You are clean, washed in the blood of the lamb." I wanted nothing more than that to become a distant memory, but it was not, and it happened again and again, as you will see. One thing that I know now, is that you have got to pray and pray because once Jesus arrives the devil must pack up his gear and leave the scene on fire' burning from the inside out. Just look at what Satan does in Job 1:7-12,

And the Lord said unto Satan, Whence comest thou? Then Satan answered the LORD, and said, from going to and fro in the earth, and from walking up and down in it. [8] And the Lord said unto Satan, "Hast thou considered my servant Job, that there is none like him in the earth, a perfect and an upright man, one that feareth God, an of his hands, avoids evil?" Then Satan answered the Lord, saying, "Has Job feared God for nothing? Have You not made a hedge around him, around his household, and around all that he has on every side? You have blessed the work of his hands, and his possessions have increased in the land. But stretch out Your hand now, and touch all that he has, and he will curse You to Your face. The Lord said to Satan, "Look, all that he has is in your power; only do not stretch out your hand against his person."

Just please understand this one major point, when you call upon JESUS, the enemy must depart from the presence of the LORD. This was not the first nor the last time that the enemy turned around in my life; this was only the beginning to Satan's destructive ways towards me, a woman with a world filled with nothing but dreams. It was for this reason that I had to let Larry go; I felt that he was dragging me down to absolute zero, and I was not a woman that could ever be considered a "nothing type" of girl. So, if you have someone who is bring you down, my suggestion to you is that you pull yourself up, brush yourselves off, and hold your head up high and walk away from that zero who thought he had found another zero and call yourself a hero for kicking that piece a trash against the curb!

I NEVER had gotten over Kelvin! My heart ached to see him so badly that I began to pray for it to happen. I want you all to know that I am accustomed to praying. I can pray all night, and God often wakes me up at 3 A.M. to pray. But there was something about Kelvin that I could not let go of, so I prayed. I woke up the next morning hoping that Kelvin would just appear at the front door of the old French colonial that I lived in off Broad Street, but he did not. I rode the bus to school, and I waited all day at school but no Kelvin. I got on the bus, and I closed my eyes and began to pray, and I said, "Lord, if I make it to my house without seeing Kelvin, I will know that it was never meant to be." I got off the bus and began to walk as my eyes filled with tears, because I was all alone as I took that walk down that lonely street. Then suddenly there is a blue VW bug pulling up beside me and, he said, "Hey, pretty, do you need a ride home?" I could not believe it; it was Kelvin, the man I had been praying that I would see all day long. I said yes, and he pulled around in the street, and I got in and he kissed me like he had been missing me too. Now, the world was alright with me again. We went to a Chinese food restaurant, and I had fried rice and sweet and sour chicken for the first time with the man that I knew was going to be my husband. We started to have a magnificent day, and the night was magical, because I was in the arms of my baby all night long. We let the window up in my room to hear all the sounds coming from the French Quarter as we slept throughout the night with smooth jazz playing on the radio. I was so in love and there was nothing that anyone could say or do about it; baby, I was in LOVE! Now, ask me, was Kelvin in love with me, and the answer would be that he probably thought that I was a very sweet country girl who needed guidance from a man, and that was something that he could provide me with, but LOVE, no, I do not believe he would have called it that. Maybe infatuation, that seems reasonable. But for the next year, all I could think about was Kelvin and how much I loved him and how he doted over me. It seemed that everything in our world was perfect. We would go out into the quarters for a late-night drink, and he would surprise me all the time and come over, and we would talk until the sun would come up, making plans for our future together. We both wanted everything that the world had to offer us, and we could laugh non-stop for hours.

But Satan was watching, and he was angry with me because of my happiness; he had to find a way back into that door of my life. He was pacing the floor, enraged at trying to develop a plan of action to destroy me. The devil really has some gall. Kelvin knew that it was my birthday, so he and some of his friends decided to throw me a party. It wasn't just any type of party, it was a "get high" party. There was liquor, beer, coolers, marijuana, and cocaine, and there was not a small amount of this but an abundance of everything. He brought two of his friends and my two roommates. Baby, did they get high! I was so shocked, because they all did cocaine, and they all drank Hennessey and all I did was smoke some weed and drink two coolers, and I was done. When I came to the next morning, Kelvin and I were lying in bed fully dressed, and he had snow all around his nose. I left him there sleeping and looked for the others, but I could not find anyone. I knew that Satan must have partied so hard, because he knew that he had kicked the door wide open and came sashaying through it. With celebratory hands, he was clapping like a little child with a brand-new bicycle. And once again he had gotten me and the whole gang of us in one swift move. I knew it was true when his boys suddenly appeared as the sun came up and Kelvin was waiting on me. He loved me, and I could see it each time I looked at him, but there was something different about the way he looked at me; it was almost as if he could see through me. He smiled at me as I walked down the stairs and asked if he could speak with me in private. I went into the kitchen and sat down, and he said this to me; he asked me would I sleep with his friend for ten thousand dollars. This was his boy who played football for an NFL team who was sitting in my living room. I stood up in total disbelief that he had asked me a question such as that one. Tears rolled down my cheeks, and I said, "No, how could you ask something like this of me?" I could see Satan sitting in a seat, on ready for my answer, rubbing his hands anxiously, and then I said, "NO!" I disappointed him so, and I told Kelvin how he had hurt me, and he said it was only a joke, and that he was trying to see if I really loved him. He said, "Now I know that you would not leave me for money. Let's get ready to go, baby girl." He hugged me so tight, but I still believe that the guy truly made him an offer. I could see on his face as Kelvin kissed me and dropped me off for school, the guy was looking and smiling at me. One thing that I do know is that the enemy did not win that day, but there were so many times that he did! Psalms 31:1-3, "In you, O Lord, do I seek refuge, may I never be ashamed, deliver me in Your righteousness. Incline Your ear to me, deliver me speedily; be my strong rock, a strong fortress to save me. For You are my rock and my fortress, for Your name's sake lead me and guide me."

Chapter V

Mister Forever

Addicted

Addicted is defined as enthusiastically devoted
to a thing or activity or in my case a person.
I am enthusiastically devoted to you.
To you, I adore your ever presence.
To you, I long for your greatness all around me.
To you, I am incapable of not thinking of your soul
entwined with my everlasting being.
To you, I cannot breathe without you blowing gently from those beautiful lips
upon me as I awake to find you holding me and looking down on me as my
eyes slowly part from a long, sensuous night with you.
To you, I am the door that does not open until you appear.
To you, I give my heart, for you have taken it away and I can't imagine hav-
ing it back in one piece without you.
You are my addiction; it is to you I have devoted my whole world to.
To you, I am enthusiastically in LOVE with U!

When I went home that summer, my grades were so poor that my mother made me sit out of school for a semester. It was the worst time of my life, and that was only what I believed. Every day was so difficult for me, and I wondered why I was so in love with Kelvin. I had been accepted at Southern University. My father constantly arguing with my mother, her crying her eyes out. I could have just run all the way to Baton Rouge, Louisiana. Until one day he lost his mind and began to beat my mother unmercifully. Until I ran into the room and stopped him, he turned his rage on me. I ran, and I grabbed a knife out of the kitchen, and my mother saw the knife, and just as I was about to stab him, my mother jumped in between us and yelled, "Stop it, Renee'! You are going to kill your daddy," and with tears in my eyes, I said, "He better not hit you one more time!" My father looked at me and told my mother it would be him or me that had to leave. My mother chose my father, and that meant I was out without a place to go. I called Kelvin and told him that I had to be gone by the time my mother left for work. That meant that Kelvin would have to drive all night long to get to me in Birmingham, Alabama. He arrived at seven o'clock in the morning, and I thought that meant that Kelvin loved me, but I would soon find out that was the exact opposite of what it meant. And my mother and father showed me about the same love as they did a dog; my mother did not ask him where he was taking me or anything. Kelvin and his friend were showering the compliments on to my mother, and she was smiling like nothing was wrong. How could she be smiling like this when my world was crumbling all around me? There were no goodbyes; there was nothing but "Call me once you get there," and I was gone.

Once I got into the car, tears started to roll down my face, and Kelvin hugged me and said that everything was going to be fine now. Somehow, I needed to believe him, and I went fast asleep. When I awoke, I was at a small apartment complex, and this was where I was, day and night, for two weeks with no communication with anyone but Kelvin who came in late at night and left early that next day. There were lots of tears shed during this time over my mother and how I felt betrayed by her actions. And then there was Kelvin, leaving me in this dark hole for whole days all alone. Oh, I forgot that sometimes there was sex, which I felt that I owed him for taking me out of that violent situation at home, and other times, there was wild, uninhibited sex as a stress relief, to calm a sister's nerves down before she lost it. I knew that this was no good, so I called Southern University to check and see if I could check in on campus, they finally said yes, I could move into my room. Relief had finally come.

Kelvin brought me to campus and put all my things in my room, and I kissed him goodbye; he said, "I will see you later." And as I was holding on to his hand, he reassured me that everything was going to be fine. I trusted him, or I just needed to trust him, because at that very moment, he was all that I had in the world.

In a matter of weeks, Kelvin's mother passed away. He seemed to be at his lowest point, and I felt every bit of his sadness. He asked me to come over, and I did what he asked of me. I arrived at his home to find him lost as a little boy. I was not expecting what came next. I was taken to a room to sit amongst a room filled with women. I immediately began to ask who they were, and they all replied they were friends of Kelvin. One young lady told me she was his girlfriend, and at that point, I got up and went outside only to find Kelvin laughing and talking with his brothers. I demanded to know what was going on, and he became so angry, he stepped to me to slap me, but his older brother stopped him. I said I am ready to go back on campus, and he said, "Find your way," and his brother said, "No, you are going to take her. Kelvin, you brought her into all of this, and you are going to take her away from it." He drove me back and not one word was shared between the two of us. I got out of the car and walked to my suite, and he drove away. I was under the impression it was over. Kelvin did not call me for days, and then there was a call, and he asked me to come to the funeral, because he needed me there, and I told him maybe I would come. I thought about it and a girlfriend of mine convinced me to go and she would go with me. She took me, and I was dressed in my pretty green-linen suit, and his other women were all dressed in black, even the chick that arrived in her private limousine. After the funeral was over, I turned to walk away, and I felt his hand touch mine and I turned, and he said, "Please, stay," as he gave me a single red rose, and then he kissed me in front of everyone. The other women who had respect for themselves got in their cars and left, but there were some that stayed. We went to the house, and he served me and my friend food and beverages, and the other women just sat and looked at us. My girlfriend had to leave, and he begged me to stay, and I stayed. He stayed in my presence all that evening, and he told me to get some clothes and come back and stay the night with him. He provided me with a car, and I went back to campus feeling like I could fly, never thinking that this was all a game; it was so real to me, and I was so thrilled. I went and changed my clothes and packed a bag, and I was off to another sham, and it did not take long for it to begin. As soon as we arrived at his apartment, there was a knock at the door, and she said, "Kelvin, let me in," and when he would not let her in, she just sat outside with the lights beaming into the windows; it was like a nightmare. He just continued to tell me to go to sleep and get some rest, everything was going to be fine. But for the first time, fine did not mean good or alright to me, it meant chaotic or confusion all around me. I remember what the word of God said in 1 Corinthians 14:33, "For God is not the author of confusion, but of peace, as in all churches of the saints." There was so much tension all around Kelvin and these women and the lifestyle in which he lived for the next two-and-a-half years, I was in one situation after another. I was once found by a girl who came to me as a friend, but she was in total inner turmoil, and she got me to go with her for something to eat, and if you know me, that is always the word to get me moving wherever you want me to go. I digress, but we got into this girl's car, and she drove to some railroad tracks, and a train was coming, and she stopped up on the tracks and put the car in park, and I said, "Hey, there is a train approaching us. Come on," and she said, "I do not care; if I cannot have Kelvin, neither can you." I said, "Wait a minute, you can have him; let's get off these tracks." She began saying no, and I told her I would call him and tell him that it was over between us. She then shifted the car into drive and pulled off the railroad tracks with only a minute to spare. I jumped out of the car, and she took off. I called Kelvin and told him about the craziness of that girl and that I was done with him and I done until he called me again and invited me to his home. Now you think that was some crazy shit? Check this out. I come over, and he greets me with a warm energetic kiss. He tells me to make myself at home, so I take off my shoes and sit on the sofa, and he brought me something to drink. We kissed some more and watched the game. There was something going on in the back, and I, of course, inquire, but before he could answer, this big, black, tall, Amazonian bitch walked right pass us to the refrigerator, got something to drink, and warmed a bottle and walked back into the bedroom. I am like, WTF is going on; he then said, "She is here, because she does not have anywhere to go, and we have a daughter." I stood up and said, "Are you CRAZY?" Putting on my shoes and screaming at him at the same time, I told him he must have been out of his motherfucking mind to bring me back into some shit like this, when he has got a child with a bitch, and she is living in the house with him! Did he believe that I was going to deal with that kind of BS? The correct answer was hell no! I got my purse and left out of the door blazing, you could see the flames coming from my head a mile away; what in the hell was he thinking? I guess that I was a fool! I pulled off from that house on two wheels! Later, I was inconsolably crying my eyes out. This nigga did this shit to me again! I am done with Kelvin!

It was a beautiful summer, and I was almost done with school, meeting new men everywhere. Having fun with them and never calling them back. It was quite liberating. Suddenly, I was partying at a club with my Caucasian friends, and I felt ice hitting me, and I was lit up by this time, and who did I see standing in the balcony? Only Kelvin. He gave me a big, bright thirty-two-teeth smile, and I put up my middle finger and continued dancing with my crew of vanilla ice. When I decided that I had enough, I called for a taxi and got dropped off at my apartment, and I lay in bed and just thought of the times that Kelvin had me in his arms. I felt as though I was finally free, and I did not know why I felt like he had me under a spell of some kind, but I was finally deinstitutionalized, but I was only lying to myself. As my life continued, you will have the opportunity to see Kelvin in and out of my life. But this I know now, as James 4:7 states, "Submit yourselves therefore to God. Resist the devil, and he will flee from you." That is all that you have to do; whenever you see someone who has been nothing but bad news for you, tell him or her hello and goodbye all in the same breath. You have to be nice, but that is it. Remember, let God fight your battle; he always comes to win, and he will win the battle; he will put them to shame.

The day of my graduation came; I finished my studies from Southern University. I was so excited about finishing up my degree in psychology. I could not wait to start my career. My family came, and my friends were there, and we all were having a great time celebrating my graduation. Down deep I was crying, because I kept hoping that Kelvin would somehow surprise me, but he didn't, and I was so sad, but I had to keep smiling. When my family left, I was glad, and I went into my room and cried and packed, tears falling over Kelvin for he had missed the most important day of my life. The next day, I would be leaving Baton Rouge. I thought for sure Kelvin would come by to see me off, but no Kelvin. Now, I was mad. I said my final goodbyes to my roommates, and I drove to Kelvin in the pouring rain. I got out of my car and ran to the door and beat on that door until my hand was just about raw. Then from nowhere, someone came from behind me and touched me, and said in the gentlest voice, "Go, he won't answer you." When I looked up, I could hardly see, but it was someone in a black poncho, and I walked away. I turned to tell him thank you and to say goodbye to Kelvin, but he was gone, but that was impossible. There was nowhere for him to go that quickly. I looked up and down the street as I backed away, but there was nothing but the sheets of rain falling as I drove back to Birmingham, torn completely apart. I felt like a satanic spirit was riding in the back seat, rolling in laughter over the way in which I had been treated, and I could not stop balling, and he could not stop laughing. I remember driving up into the driveway and getting out of the car and ringing the doorbell and my mother saying, "What in the world happened to you?" And me saying, "Nothing," as I went into my room and took off my clothes and put on a night gown and just slept. I woke up on Monday morning; I slept from Saturday afternoon until Monday. All I could remember was being inconsolable. But what I did not know is stated in Joshua 23:3, "And ye have seen all that the Lord your God hath done unto all these nations because of you; for the Lord and your God is he that hath fought for you." You see not only does God fight our battles, he also protects us from harm. I was crying, because after all that we had been through, how could Kelvin not open the door for me? And I do believe that God sent one of his angels to tell me to go, and that was God's way of watching over me, because who knows what would have happened if someone on the other side of that door would have become angry and acted out in an irrational manner. People, if something tells you that it is not the right thing to do, DO NOT DO IT and JUST WALK AWAY! Because the enemy is looking for a good laugh at, guess whose expense, yours; don't let him win!

Chapter VI

Floridian Craze

I had my first job in the great state of Florida. I loved the sunny skies, hot weather, and beautiful beaches. Most of all I was away from my father; he was the same man that I had left behind when I went away to college, and I could not bear to stay in that house with him, so I took the first job that was offered to me, and it was in Tampa Bay. My mother and I drove to Tampa; we talked and laughed all the way to Brooksville. My mom was and will always be my BFF. I still loved my mommy, no matter what had happened between us; it was all in the past.

I worked at a juvenile detention for boys who had been given their last chance before being sent to prison. These were some terrible young men, but you would never guess it, because they had been busy keeping that mask on for the public to see. I saw some awful things while I was there; it is true that they will make the weak ones their bitches, and this goes for all of them. Most of them had a story to tell about their childhood, that is if you could get them to open up and to share their nightmare of a childhood.

I called the guys in my group my little boys. They all had a special place in my heart. They told me that I needed to get out, and they knew just the place, and they sent me to a club in Tampa. So, Saturday night I got dressed in my nicest black-linen, backless dress and went to the club; to my surprise, the club was down a dark road, and it was a hole in a wall. When I went inside, it was so dark, and there were guys everywhere. There was this one guy who was so drunk he could hardly stand up, but he insisted upon talking with me. He told me that he could not buy me a drink, and all I wanted to say was, "Go the hell away from me now." After, I had tried to convince him that his friend would like him to sit with him, and he said no, he could not leave a beautiful girl all alone in a place where there were so many rats prowling all around. So, I finally said I would leave, and he gave me a napkin with his name and number on it. I took it and said good night. When I returned to work, my boys all wanted to know, did I meet anyone, and I told them all no. Who wanted to admit to meeting someone who was drunk? Not I. But I could not help but to think of him; he was tall, and I guess, handsome, if you could catch him without a glass of vodka in his hand. So, I went and searched through my evening bag and found his number; his name was Antwan. I called, and he answered the phone, and all that I said was, hello and he said, "I knew that you would call me." He immediately asked me out, and I said yes. On the night we went out, I was embarrassed, because I did not have any furniture. I was sleeping on a pallet, which is several quilts on the floor, and my addition was a homemade Delta Sigma Theta comforter and two pillows. And he sat at the bar on one of the two stools that I had bought, and I was very proud of them, because I bought them with money that I had earned from my very first check after finishing college. And he told me that it was okay and that I would get some more furniture soon. I have to tell you that this man had on a shiny, pink polyester shirt and some black pants that he had just bought from some little shop. I knew right then that we should not be going out, because we were unequally yoked, and it warns against this when in 2 Corinthians 6:14, "Be ye not unequally yoked with unbelievers: for what fellowship hath righteousness with unrighteous? And what communion hath light with darkness?" We went out to have dinner and a movie and he was trying to be as nice as possible. I could see that we were not cut from the same cloth, but in my eyes that did not matter.

Antwan was always such a nice guy; he showed me Tampa, and it was great. He soon asked me to marry him, and of course, I said yes. Shortly after that I noticed a change; he became somewhat demanding of me. I did not mind it; I was busy planning for my wedding with my mom. As my date was rapidly approaching, one night Antwan came over to my apartment so drunk he could barely walk. I refused to let him in and that enraged him. He became so belligerent with me that I slammed the door in his face, and as he walked away cursing me, all of a sudden, I heard a huge sound of cursing and tumbling and cursing as he rolled down the stairs. I was afraid he might be dead. As I opened the door, all that I saw was him standing up, brushing himself off, and him saying, "SHIT!" as he staggered around searching for his keys. At this point, I knew that he was okay, and I burst into tears and laughter as I could not breathe with the images of him rolling down those stairs. As I watched him from my window, he got into that "piece of crap of a car," as he called it, and drove away; there was a place in my mind, that said, "Do you really want to marry a man like this?" But I pushed that out of my head, but looking back today, I realize that the small soft voice was God's way of attempting to talk to me and trying to draw my attention away from Antwan to me. You see, I am also involved in this scenario, and my true father's thoughts were of me and what I really needed. God knew that I was making a mistake that I could never walk away from; this was my first red flag not to marry Antwan.

For the next few months, before we were to be married and after his drunken rage, he was such a sweetheart. You see, it is just like the devil to hide out in plain sight, by being someone that you would never suspect of him, in this case, a sweet and gentle man, which Antwan was not. But I never even took notice of how sweet he had become until we left for Birmingham, and I actually told my mother that Antwan was such a sweet man. And right before our wedding, we were going to pick up the tuxedos with the family, and I said, "Antwan, you are going in the wrong direction," and he snapped. He told me to shut the fuck up and that I talked too fucking much. I was waiting on his mom or dad to say something, but they said nothing, and I sat there with tears rolling down my face. My second red flag not to marry Antwan. I am going to ask you here, is something like this happening to you, or has this ever happened to you? Then you need to STOP and take a good hard look at the relationship that you are in and begin to pray and seek the Lord God's face. Don't wait to bring it before the Lord for an answer.

The next day was my wedding day. I was so confused, but I did not know the scripture that says, "For God is not the author of confusion, but of peace, as in all churches of the saints." (1 Corinthians 14:33) I did not know what this scripture meant. It means that God is not ever in the presence of any form of confusion or chaos. But now that I do, I would not have made the decision to marry Antwan, for he was like a cartoon character that, as children, we knew as Slept Rock. Slept Rock was a character who walked with a cloud of rain and thunderstorms over his head, and always there was so much confusion with him that it always was wowed me; this was Antwan's life. This was the man that I sat in the limousine, all dressed up, on my wedding day, contemplating whether I should go through with this marriage. As I watched an old friend of mine enter into the door, my heart raced. The driver said, "You know, you do not have to do this; I will take you home or anywhere that you want to go," but I smiled and told him to come around and open the door. The rest of the day was all a blur. All I remember was the photographer on our very last photo of the day telling Antwan, "Would you, please, just smile," and he could not do it save his life. This memory was buried so deep in my mind that I could not dig it out until now. After we had consummated the marriage, I looked over at Antwan sleeping, and said, "My God, what have I done? What in the world have I done?"

What Have You Done?

What have you done, U silly Girl?
U went out and married a man, or maybe a boy.
Oh my God, U silly girl!
Does this man really know who you are, or better yet, does this man really, really Love U?
U can make such rash and stupid decisions, u r such a silly girl.
Does he even know whom he is himself?
What in the world have you done, you silly little girl?
Is there anyone, anywhere that really cares about you?
U took a leap of faith, and now you are falling from Heaven's secret hiding place, you are such a silly, silly girl.
Nothing left to do but cry yourself to sleep, and think of all the people that will call you a silly, silly little girl for what U have done...

My days following wedding day were days of trying to please Antwan and tears that would follow because of his constant barrage of abusive language and him taking money from me without me knowing anything about it or him attempting to beat me in front of his parents, who said or did absolutely nothing to help me. It was like they wanted him to beat me so that I would succumb to his outrageous way of thinking, but the God in me would not let me do it. I remember a discussion I had with my mother, and I was really hurting and wanting to leave Antwan, and she said this to me, "Take a good look at yourself first, and if you do not see anything that you are doing, then you can go, but take a hard look at yourself first, because it could be you Renee'." I felt so alone and ashamed. And then I looked at myself, and I could not see anything that I was doing wrong. I was trying all the time to be the perfect wife. There was something about what my mother had said to me, in looking at myself, that I did not know if she meant to take a look at me, because that might actually help me to make a decision on whether to leave him, or to take a look at me, because I was the destructive one. But that day was soon to come where I had to take a good, long, hard look in the mirror at myself or be six feet under without any introspection.

I remember this day like it was yesterday, I had gotten my first real promotion, and my pay was substantially higher. I was so excited; I came home a little earlier and met Antwan and a friend drunk, and they were still drinking. I told them about my promotion, and Antwan's friend was so happy for me. I asked him if he did not mind that Antwan and I were going out to celebrate, and he said of course not, but Antwan begged him to stay, but he left anyway, saying congratulations to me. When Antwan shut the door, all hell broke loose, it was not Antwan anymore. I tried to say something, but Antwan interrupted with a violent outburst saying, "You are the very BITCH that I do not want to be with anymore." It was like the devil rose up and was standing right in front of my eyes. All I can recall was being slapped down to my knees and him jumping on top of me, choking me; I remember feeling like I was so cold, and Antwan all of a sudden, stopped choking me and just shook me until I woke up coughing, and he picked me up and carried me into the bedroom. And he told me that he was not himself, that something came over him, and that he could feel himself choking me, and then there were my tears running down my face that stopped him, because he felt the warmth of them and the coldness of my body, and he knew that I was dying. It felt like the Satan was just standing in a corner of my bedroom, watching with an angry smirk on his face saying,

"You should have killed the BITCH!" I could not speak at that moment, but once I was able to, I told Antwan that he had to go, because if he hated me that much, I would be dead the next time. Antwan begged me to stay, but I said no; I told him to leave. When my roommate came home, she called for me, and I could barely answer her. When she came into the room, she was being silly and her cheerful self, and she jumped onto the bed with me, and I screamed. She looked at me with those big eyes and said, "I am sorry. What's wrong?", and with tears in my eyes, I showed her my neck and all I can remember was her saying, "OMG what happened?" and I could barely tell her due to the pain, but I got the words out, and she said, "Let's call the police," and I said no, but I should have done that, but instead I just laid upon Linda's shoulder and cried myself to sleep. The next morning, I went in to work with a scarf around my neck, and when the day was over, I went home to find my closet was cleaned out and the key was on the dining room table. I cried and cried until I could not cry any more. And just remember, like I should have remembered, to cast all your anxiety on him, because he CARES FOR YOU (US). Be alert, sober mind. Your enemy, the devil, prowls around like a roaring lion looking for someone to devour. Resist him, standing firm in the faith, because you know that the family of believers throughout the world is undergoing the same kind of sufferings. 1 Peter 5:7-9.

Chapter VII

What the Enemy Meant for Evil, God Meant It for GOOD (Genesis 50:20)

When I decided to write about these situations in my life, I realized that this was the enemy's way of trying to break me down to nothing. He let me encounter being raped on four different occasions. I thought I would lose my mind, but only my Lord Jesus saw me through these terrible attacks on my flesh as the enemy tried to destroy my spirit. See these were weak men that had defiled my body, but something in me said that they were strong, so much stronger than me. Our Lord knew what he was doing; he knew that I had a story to tell, and once I was awakened, that this story was going to come out and find so many young women who have been through the same thing as me, and they needed someone who could tell them how they could survive it all. I cried out to God both day and night, and I never gave up; although my body was tired, I continued to call on Jesus. "And call upon me in the day of trouble: I will deliver thee, and thou shalt glorify me." Psalm 50:15

I never reported any of them; this is the first time that I have shared this with anyone other than my mother. I regret that I did not go to an authority figure and report what had happened to me; I just sat back and wallowed in my emotional pain while Satan sat and watched me and he laughed at me. I was torn apart each time, and I didn't understand why this had happened to me. I was totally perplexed by what these men could have been thinking, what could have been running through their minds, and I can only conclude that the enemy had taken total control over them, and you know a man that has lost his soul to Satan when he has been thinking negative thoughts, been jealous, been stealing, or cheating, then they have given Satan plenty of room to come in and snatch their soul. That is what I believe happened to these men. The enemy sits in a corner, watches and waits until you leave the door cracked open, and then he sticks his toe right in, and then he shows up, unexpectedly, and takes total control.

The first time that I was raped, it was when I was a teenager. It was so damaging to me, emotionally and physically, that I tried to forget it ever happened, but God would not let me leave it behind, because he knew what he had planned for my life, and I would be in need of it. So, let's begin. I met this handsome guy at church. He did not look like there was anyone that he meant any harm. His girlfriend was a beautiful young lady, but she seemed as though she did not care about him. My feelings were correct, because she broke up with him. I was available, and Fredrico came running to be with me; it started out nice. He took me to my formal dance, and it was okay. Whereas it should have been wonderful; that was God giving me a sign, but I went right past that, didn't even notice it. I was young, and I was what I thought in love. By now my parents were trusting Fredrico, and I asked them if I could go out on a date with Fredrico and their answer was yes. I was so excited I could hardly breathe. When I told Fredrico, he said we were going to a movie. I was so overwhelmed with joy that I couldn't wait. The night finally came, and Fredrico arrived, and I told my parents that he was there, and I said goodbye to them, never thinking a thing was going to happen. I told him hello, and he began to drive, never talking much, but when I saw him going in the wrong direction, I questioned him, and he pulled into a motel. I said, "Why are we here?" and he said, "We will only stay a few minutes." I reluctantly said okay. I was walking to the room door slowly, and he said, "Come on," so I entered the door, and he shut it behind me. I knew right there I had made the worst mistake of my life. He sat down on the bed and started to kiss me on my neck, and I told him that he should stop. But he refused and he pushed me down on to the bed, and I said, "Please, don't do this," but he did not stop, and I closed my eyes and just prayed that it didn't happen, but I felt him enter me, and the tears just ran down my face. I lay there, with tears streaming down my face, as he devoured my treasure, taking every part of me and not letting go. The enemy was there in the room, taunting him, telling him, "Go on; she is nothing but a useless little girl. Take what you want; it is yours," and laughing out loud like a mad man. When Fredrico finished, he got up, washed himself off, and told me to come on, and he took me home, never saying a word. It seemed like he was a hungry beast that had totally devoured his prey. I never told anyone other than my mother at a much older age. I have seen him at church where I got out of his way. I never talked to him again. He hurt me so bad emotionally that I would lie in bed and cry about what was done to me. Physically, I had to wear bandages over my breast for weeks so that they would heal properly afterwards. I was scared to tell anyone about what had happened to me, because I knew that no one would believe me; I had fallen prey to this demonic-filled man. Have you been tortured by a man that you once looked up to, and everyone liked him because they did not know who he really was or what he was capable of doing? It is a betrayal of character that is misleading women all over the world, and it is Satan who chooses to play this game with the hearts of women that God has anointed for his purpose to gratify them to fulfill their destiny.

My second encounter with this demonic force was when I moved to Tennessee. I came, not expecting anything, because I had left an abusive marriage that had torn me down physically with the beatings and mentally with the horrible verbal abuse. I was just looking for relaxation. I met a young woman who was the life of the party. She liked me, and she invited me to all of her parties. I always thought she just wanted to see me smile, because I was always so unhappy. One evening, after work, she said that she was going to have a little social, and she asked me to come; of course, I said yes, and I was there. Everyone was drinking and having a good time mingling and socializing, and then there was a knock at the door, and who walks in but the most beautiful black man I had ever seen. He saw Kay Kay, and he squeezed her tight and gave her a peck on the cheek. I was sitting there in awe of his presence, and then it happened, she walked over to me and introduced him to me; I must have said something, but I could not remember. I was absolutely taken with him. I asked Kay Kay if she was talking with him; she said no and told me I should call him, and she gave me his office number. I was so excited I could not wait to speak with him.

I could not finish work soon enough, but I did, and I was out of that office with a lightening on my feet. I called him, and once I had arrived home, he said he remembered me. And that made me all the happier. He was a little arrogant, so I thought, he spoke of himself and all the business he was doing since he was no longer playing pro football. I did not let that bother me; I went right on, and when he said we could get dinner, I said okay. Saturday night could not come quick enough, and I was ecstatic about my dinner date with Maurice. There was a knock at the door, and when I opened the door, I smiled. He just came in and plopped down on to my sofa, my puppy came over to him, and he just grabbed him up and you could see the fear in Pequito. I took Pequito and put him in his cage. When I came back, he asked me for a glass of water, I went to get it for him and returned; he was standing. He took the glass from me, and he drank the water and sat the glass down. He called for me to come to him, and I said, "Are you ready to go?" And he said, "Just come here," so I did. When I got close, he yanked my arm and bent me over the sofa, and pulled up my skirt as I screamed, he said, "Shut up, you know you want it." Then he pulled my panties to one side and forced himself inside of me. As tears streamed down my face, he finished up, and I got up and he said, "Stop, you know you wanted it. I got to go," and he walked out the door, leaving me there with my treasure having been stolen away from me once again. Never wanting this to happen to me, I was wondering why God had let this happen to me again. I went upstairs totally despondent; I did not talk or leave my house for three days. I could not say much of anything to anyone for a couple of weeks. Has someone ever hurt you so badly that you cannot seem to breathe? I could not breathe whenever I thought of what had happened to me; it was awful and by a man that could have any woman that he wanted, and who would ever believe me? No one, if I cried rape. They would say that I wanted him so badly, and he would never even talk to me. So, I never told anyone anything about that night until many, many years later. I kept it inside, all bundled up where no one could see the pain that was eating me up from the inside outward. When was the last time you spent the day in prayer and healing your wounds that no one ever knew about but you? It takes a lot of green tea and meditation to get past that sort of traumatic event in your life.

When I came back to my Birmingham home, and I stayed for a while, after having left the CDC and deciding to do something else that I loved. So,

I decided to sell, and I started with furniture. I sold furniture in a major furniture store in Five Points West. It was a nice store, and I loved working with the decorator of the store. I would often be in the window with her on my down time. On this particular day, a tall, handsome man came into the store and asked for the young lady in the window. Everyone knew that it was me; they all called for me. I was surprised to see this tall, handsome guy. I introduced myself and he introduced himself as Pastor Tommy Seal; I asked him what he was looking for. He told me a bedroom suite. I was excited to show him around, and we finished up on the mattress; he tried out my favorite, and we sat there, and I gave him a total. He told me that he would be back to get it, and I said that would be great. He had been flirting with me the entire time, and before he left, he asked me for my number, and I gave it to him. He asked me, "Could we go out?" and I said, "That would be nice." So, once he left the store, everyone wanted to tell me who he was and that he had his own church. The young women that worked with me said, "He likes you"; they thought they could see it in his eyes, but they would have never guessed what happened next.

"Beware of false prophets, who come to you in sheep's clothing, but inwardly they are ravenous wolves." (Matthew 7:15) I had tried to find someone to babysit for my son (my son will be discussed later), but I could not find anyone to watch him. So, I told Pastor Seal, and he said that would be good, he enjoyed children. He came over, and I had given my son a bath, and he was ready for bed within thirty minutes of Tommy's arrival. I read him a bedtime story, and he was fast asleep. I went back into the living room with Tommy, and his whole personality had changed. He appeared so arrogant; I tried to sit next to him, and he said, "Get up, and let's go to your bedroom." I said no, and then he grabbed my arm and said, "You best do what I say, or I will hurt your pretty little boy." He closed my baby's door, and we went into my room where he pushed me down and told me to take off my panties. I said no, and he said, "Do you really want something to happen to that kid?" So, I took them off, and he got on top and immediately shoved himself inside of me, and all I can remember was his hot breath on my neck as the tears ran down my face. When he was done, he got up and said thank you and left my apartment just like nothing happened. I went and checked on my son immediately, but he was sleeping. I went and got in the shower and rubbed my skin so hard that you would have thought that someone had poured something poisonous on me, but it was me feeling like I had lost my treasure to yet another man. And the tears fell, and I cried till my face and eyes were just swollen shut. I cannot tell you how deeply that man hurt me; it felt like I was nothing! I was just empty for about two years; I can't remember what happened to my life during that timeframe. And you know what else? No one ever noticed that I was hurting on the inside; I do know I gained a lot of weight. Have you ever been lost, and no one knew where you were but God? And have you ever felt like the enemy was just sitting in a corner with his legs crossed, just with a smirk on his face, and taking one puff after another on a cigarette saying, "NOW WHAT U GONNA DO?" Back then I did not know God like I do now, because he would have had to go, because I know what stirs him out of his pants, and that is calling on the name of JESUS! When he is somewhere, he should not be calling on Jesus, "submit yourselves therefore to God. Resist the devil, and he will flee from you." (James 4:7)

"My Cries"

There was a day I cried all night long until I could barely see for my eyes were filled with tears of pain from a Woman who had been raped so violently that her breast felt like they were come apart in pain.
For the enemy had come to take my destiny through pain so deep that it had begun to shut me up and slowly but steadily drown the talents that God placed on the inside of me.
And I cried!
One man forcefully had stolen my treasure from me.
There was a day I cried all night long until I could barely see for my eyes were filled with tears of pain, for there was another who wrestled me down;
I tried, but the power of the enemy overtook me, and I lost.
Once again had stolen my treasure
And again, I cried.
The enemy came wearing a disguise, playing a role that he knew
I had been waiting for, but it was all a lie.
He threatened me and scared me.
And then he stole my treasure.

And again, I cried all night long and that is when I heard
that small still calming voice say, "Stop crying.
It is time for you to rise up and to take a stand for your destiny is at hand.
My angels are on their way and you will retain your destiny," "for the battle
is not yours, but it is the Lord's." (2 Chronicles 20:15)

Chapter VIII
Gorgeous, Is His Name

I was assigned to the Memphis clinic. I arrived there filled with hope that I would prosper. I had been told by upper management that I would be a supervisor, and I continued to work as though everyone had their eyes on me. There was an older white man over the program that liked me, but I only wanted to work for him, but he was insistent that I knew his intentions. I came into the office early, as I often did, and he was there; he came up behind me and put his nose up against my neck and startled me, and he whispered, "You smell so good. What fragrance are you wearing?" My response was "You are invading my personal space. Please, don't do that again." He got so angry with me; he walked away furious. You could see it all over his face. From that point on, it was a living hell to work up under his leadership. I became so ready to leave the organization that I applied for a supervisory position in Los Angeles. I interviewed for the position and was told after the interview that I had given the most comprehensive answer, and they assured me that I would be given the job. I heard nothing from the personnel office. So, I took it that I was not hired. After many years had passed, I went to a conference and ran into one of the men that sat on the board, and he told me what had happened. He told me that my Director had spoken with the interviewing board and told them that I did terrible work, and I started problems and that they should not hire me. That was what had been done, and I went to my room and cried all night.

But what I did not remember in the word it says, "whosoever diggeth a pit will fall into it, and he that rolleth a stone, it will return upon him." (Proverbs 26:27) The devil sat and watched this all play out, and he laughed and laughed about it, and my heart was broken into pieces. I was hurt so bad when they did not call me back. I could not believe it, what had I done wrong for them not to give me an answer? As time went by, I got accustomed to the environment that I was forced to reside in, and I made friends. We laughed and had a good time; Memphis turned out to be a nice spot.

I met some very handsome guys, but there was one that was absolutely gorgeous, and I had what I thought was the opportunity to date this gorgeous man. He could see that I liked him a lot and I guess he took advantage of my kindness and took it for a weakness. I would always call him after work and invite him over for dinner, not that I was going to cook, it was taking out every time. If I would have cooked him anything, he would have slapped his grandmama. That something that we say in the south, but really and truly, I can cook. Now where was I? Oh, I know, I was telling you about always inviting him over, and he would always come. But one of these nights we had a long talk about this woman that he had been involved with, and she had a son for him, but she was a married woman. I comforted him and told him that everything was going to be okay. He and I begin to kiss each other, and one thing led to another, and we stayed up all night listening to jazz on the radio and him touching my face like he loved me. The next morning, when we got up, he told me that I would make such a good girlfriend, but I was just too dark for him. I stood in the door with my mouth open as he kissed me and strolled down the stairs, I could not believe that he would say such a thing to me. I walked inside and began to laugh; it was actually funny to me. And at that very moment, my past experiences started to play over again in my head. I was too dark to be a wife to the first man I had ever loved; I was too dark to become a world-renowned journalist; I was too dark for the world to want to watch me on television, just STOP! I could not do this to myself again! I decided to block every thought, and I ran and got into the shower and off I went to work. But there were always thoughts creeping up in my mind. I had to let go of those terrible, heart-wrenching situations that were causing me unbearable pain. What I had to remember, and you also need to, is that Satan is a dishonorable being, for it says, "Ye are your father the devil, and the lust of your father ye will do: he was a murderer from the beginning, and abode not in the truth, because there is not truth in him. When he speaketh a lie, he speaketh of his own: **for he is a liar**, and the father of it." (John 8:44)

I thought that I was through with him, but low and behold, I found out that I was pregnant. I had been told that I would never conceive a child, but here I was, pregnant with a child for a man that clearly did not want anything to do with me. When I told him, he was furious; he told me to have an abortion immediately, and I told him to go to hell, that I was having my baby, because I had been told that I could not have any children, and God had blessed me with this child that I was going to have my baby. He told me that I was on my own, and he was done with me, but I did not believe him, but he turned his back to me and kept walking. I can remember sitting in my closet, filled with clothes and a hundred twenty-two pairs of shoes and just balling like a baby, because I was hurting. I almost lost my baby, and it was due to my baby having so much of his father's blood that he was rejecting mine, but we survived it all. I remember my mother and father came to stay with me until I felt better, and Mr. Gorgeous called me and asked could he come over, and I said he could not come to meet my family, because he did not want me. Why should he want to meet my parents? And I just hung up. My father kept me laughing the whole time that they were there; he told my mother that I had a damn basket for everything under the counter. He said that I was just like my momma; I kept a house spotless, and I had him afraid to sit down on anything. He was a funny man. They left me, but not without my mother telling me she was just a phone call away, and she would drag my daddy out of the house with her. He told me to slow down and not to be moving so fast and then they left me to be alone in all of my emotions. I did not let my feelings rule my caring for the life that was growing inside of me. I cared for my baby by showing him all the love and concern possible. I had some great friends during my pregnancy that were both black and white; you see, even back in the day, color did not matter, only how you treated people counted, and I was sweet to everyone. You see, my life has been filled with emotional ups and downs, but if you would look past all the hurts and just praise God, he will make everything alright.

My baby's father got no better, and he walked completely out of my life and left me all alone. I turned to the only person that I knew wanted a baby as much as I did, and that was my ex-husband, and I lied and told him that the baby was his, because we had made love that one time when he was passing through, but I knew the truth. He was so happy and excited, and we spent so much time together; it was like I had imagined our marriage would have been if we could have conceived. I remember we took a road trip to Houston, and he told me stories of his father and the house that they owned in Florida. He had me laughing so hard that my belly was just going up and down as he spoke in his father's voice. He was hilarious, and I once really did love him. Before I knew it, I had fallen so in love with the little precious baby inside of me. My baby was so strong that, once, I fell asleep in the beauty salon, and my little unseen miracle began to kick so hard that he had my shirt flying up in the air, and the people around me became so afraid, because they had never seen anything like it. When my beautician woke me, I was like, "Where is everyone?" She said with a smile on her face that they moved away from you, because your baby had your shirt going up in the air he was kicking so hard. I told her that I believed that an angel was in my stomach, and they were just being boys and rough housing it a bit, Lol! My beautician just laughed and laughed! The laughs that I shared made my pregnancy bearable; I was constantly laughing at night. I would watch old episodes of *Lucy* and *Sanford and Son* and just laugh and laugh to keep myself in a joyous place. So, no matter where you are, or what you are going through, fill your world with positive people and activities that make you laugh out loud, and before you know it, God has bestowed upon you some of his grace and mercy, and you are walking through the pouring rain!

Finally, finally, it was time for my baby, and I was doing this with or without Mr. Gorgeous. I had no choice; my baby was on his way. I was scared and excited at the same time. My sister had tried to come, and I told her no, I am not having this baby until it is time but, oh no, the baby was on his way. My mother and father were on their way and so was Antwan. But my baby could not wait, after thirteen hours and me holding my breath during every labor pain, my baby arrived, and the doctor said, "Oh, he is beautiful," and all of sudden, he squirted her, and she burst into laughter saying, "I guess that works." She let me hold him, and he was the most beautiful baby I had ever seen. The nurse took him; they had to put him in the incubator to give him some oxygen, because I had deprived him of breathing for so long, he was pale. My family had arrived, and they were so excited to see Jay; my father said, "My grandboy is so fine. He is going to be my main little man."

Antwan arrived, and he was asking me if I was okay, and I said, "Yes, I am."
He asked me where was Jay, and the nurse took him to see Jay. He went to see
him, and when he came back, he was just overwhelmed with joy, and he was
saying thank you for giving me a beautiful baby boy. My eyes were open and
all that I could see was the gratitude in him; he finally had the son that he had
always wanted. We spent two days in the hospital, and the more I looked at
my son, the more he did not look like Antwan, but I prayed and asked God to
give me a son that was meant to be Antwan's, but my God could not do this
for me. I was giving him his bath, and I noticed his birth mark was in the same
location and was the same as his father, and Antwan was not his father. My
God, how was I going to tell Antwan this? This was the most difficult decision
that I had ever been given. The bible says, "for you shall know the truth and
the truth shall set you free." (John 8:32) What would you have done if you
were in this dangerous situation, knowing the type of man that Antwan was
and having to take away a gift such as his baby boy? I was released from the
hospital, and I could not keep it any longer. As I sat on the bed, I begin to cry,
and Antwan sat down beside me and asked me why was I crying, and I told him
that my little precious baby was not his, and he stood up and he said, "Who is
he; where is he?" and "WTF?" He said, "He looks like me; are you sure? He
looks like me! He is my son; he is my son! Got damn it, WTF have you done!"
He grabbed his coat and left the house in an outrage! I just sat there, balling
my eyes out. So, ladies be cautious with the men you give your love to, it is a
GIFT from God not to be shared with everyone. Mistakes like the one I made
can cost you a lifetime of pain. I hope that you all are hearing me!

Now this is where the complication really began over a pretty baby, be-
cause my boy was beautiful, but his father did not want any part of a baby. He
was going to see him if nothing else; I took him to Mr. Gorgeous, Nigel's, of-
fice. When I walked in the office, as soon as he saw Jay, you could see his over-
whelming admiration for his child, and he said, "Come to your daddy, little
man." He could not take his eyes off his son; he just wanted me to know how
beautiful he was and how glad he was that I had brought him to see him. I told
him about the birthmark that Jay had, and he immediately looked to see if I
was being truthful, and he said, "I can't believe this." I told him that I had
asked God for the child to look exactly like his father, even down to the birth-
mark so that there could be no denying him. He laughed, because he was an

atheist, and this means he did not believe in God. He doubted everything that I told him that was going to happen, and I said, "If you don't do right by Jay and I, there is nothing that will go right in your life," and he began to laugh out loud and he called me Ceily from *The Color Purple* and told me to quit putting that bad mouth on him, and he laughed so loud that you could almost see the devil stand up on the inside of him. I warned him of my father's love for me. I told him that all I wanted to do was love him and that was all his son was going to ever want was his love. He did not understand that you can't mistreat a child of God; in fact, none of the men in my life understood this principle of God. They all felt like they had escaped the wrath of my father, Jesus. It says in Matthew 18:1-6,

> "At that same time the disciples went unto Jesus, saying, who is the greatest in the kingdom of heaven? And Jesus called a little child unto him and set him in the midst of them. And said, 'Verily I say unto you, except ye be converted, and become as little children, ye shall not enter into the kingdom of heaven. Who so ever therefore shall humble himself as this little child, the same is greatest in the kingdom of heaven. And whoso shall receive one such little child in my name receiveth me. But whoso shall offend one of these little ones which believe in me, it was better for him that a millstone was hanged about his neck, and that he was drowned in the depth of the sea.'"

So, my friends, please do not worry, because one thing that I know is that God has you. Jesus carried you when you were too tired to take one more step. Let me share something with you that proves that my God has us in the palm of his hand. When I was pregnant with Jay, I had moved out to Covington, that is one of the suburbs in Memphis, it was about thirty minutes from where I worked. The traffic was terrible, but I had to drive to work and back home. So, one day, I was so tired coming home that I remember I fell asleep at the wheel, and when I woke up, I was at my exit. I don't remember driving at all, but it was like someone saying, "Wake up, you're here," and this didn't happen once but on several different occasions. So, I know that God's got you because he had me and still does. No matter what, he is with you and I all the time. Pray, trust, and believe!

My thoughts of Antwan were that he was gone for good. I thought he hated me so much, but somehow, he chose to forgive me. He came back with a plan for us to move away from Memphis and for me to leave the CDC. I was so hurt behind Nigel that I agreed. I had gotten a job working with the city of Houston and supposedly working with Antwan's family business, which never came to pass. I was taking my baby to a childcare giver's home before the day in the morning and picking my baby up after dark. I was in so much traffic that it was unbelievable. I never knew where Antwan was; he was supposed to be working. I was soon to find out that he wasn't doing anything with his time; he wasn't working. I never knew what he was doing. When it came time to pay the bills, he could not give me nothing. After two months of not knowing what was going on with him and not receiving any funds from him, I decided to move. My baby was in a home with a woman that smoked, and I was done. Antwan wanted to argue and tell me that I was not going to leave him in our apartment; I said the devil is a liar! I told him either he would drive me back, or I would tow my car behind a rental truck and drive myself back to Birmingham. He finally said that he would drive us, and he left me and my son in Birmingham, promising me that he would come back for me. Antwan came back once, and he left after being in Birmingham two weeks, and then he was gone, never to return to Birmingham again. He didn't do anything much for Jay and neither did Nigel. So, I raised my son on my own with the help of my parents and my sister. My world was changed overnight.

My father had done so much to my mother by this time that she had divorced him, and he had married another woman, and that woman who tried to reap havoc over our family's household had died of unknown causes all of a sudden. God's justice is fair and swift. My father was down and had nowhere to go. He was sick, and my sister and brother were married and I was not, so it was like I was supposed to take care of my father, and trust me, people, I did not want to have anything to do with providing him with care; he had taken my family through it all of our lives. He had damn near killed my mother on two separate occasions. But I could not walk away from him, and he loved my son, and my son loved his grandfather. They were thick as thieves per say. My dad would pick up my son from daycare and supposedly took him home but took him to the shot house every day. Once I went there, everybody in the shot house said, "Hey, Jay, what's up little man?" I was shocked to death. I asked my father about it, and he said the boy had to learn to count. I said, "Learn to count? What does him going to the shot house and counting have to do with each other?" He laughed and said, "He has a seat at the card table, and he helps me play spades. That's how he learned to count so well, and he learned some other valuable street language." I just SMH, and my father and I just laughed and laughed!

My father was going through it; he was on dialysis, he had a triple bypass, he had Sirois of the liver, and they had found throat cancer and had to get most of his teeth pulled before they could proceed with surgery to remove the cancerous growth, but I began to pray, and even the surgeon prayed, and she was an atheist, and when they went in to my father's throat, the cancer was gone. The surgeon said she could not believe it, but I knew that God would do it, because I asked him to, and he had to prove something to that young woman, that it was not all her skills and abilities but what he had given her. God was giving my father one more chance to make it right. God was letting my father have it; he had done so many bad things to so many people. But my son was his grandpa's biggest fan; he would sit outside with my father while he smoked and tell him, "Grandpa, you should not smoke. It is so bad for you. Don't you want to stay here with me for a long time?" My father would always laugh and tell Jay, "Your grandpa is going to live until he dies," and he would just laugh, but my baby would always be so upset with his grandfather for making that type of comment.

I was really having a difficult time paying all of my bills, and I had mentioned it to my father, and he said that he did not know how, but he was going to help me with my bills. I said, "Daddy, you are so funny; stop trying to think of things to make me happy. I will get through this just like before." And then I looked at my father's face and said, "Daddy, have you been to dialysis?" My father laughed, and he said, "I haven't been in a week," then he said, "Go on and tell me, call me pumpkin head or big head; go ahead," and I just laughed and laughed. And I just said, "Pumpkin head, when will you be going to dialysis, sir?" And he laughed and laughed and said, "I am going on tomorrow." I remember him saying, as he walked away, "I am going to find a way to help you Renee'," and I smiled and said, "Okay, Daddy, good night."

After I moved my father into an assisted living apartment, one dreary Saturday morning, we got a phone call from the nurse where my dad went to dialysis, and she sounded like she was crying, but she told me that we needed to come over to dialysis right away. I said to her, "What is wrong?" and she just said that we needed to be at dialysis right away and to please hurry. Me and my sister left immediately. When we got there, everyone was crying, and the doctor and nurse pulled us into the room and told us our father had passed; he had a heart attack. The nurse said he went quickly, and he was happy when he came in and had all of the patients laughing. We smiled, and they let us see him. My sister took it the hardest; she was always my daddy's favorite. I cried but not nearly as much as my sister; it was like someone took a part of her heart. I held her hands and tried to console her, but she was inconsolable. Now we had to make the final arrangements and say goodbye to only man that I knew as Daddy.

As I began to prepare for my father's funeral, the first thing I thought of was what my father was going to be wearing. Naturally, I thought of Nigel and his wonderful, handmade shirts. So, I called and told him of my father's passing, and I told Nigel I needed one of his phenomenal shirts, and it would look good on my fahter even in death; because I had never seen a man look as gorgeous in a shirt than one that had been designed by Nigel. But his answer was no, no he would not do it and gave me a million fucking reasons why he could not do it, and I told him that was okay, when I really wanted to say, "You asshole. My daddy just passed away," but instead I said okay. He could have given my daddy one of the unused or returned shirts. I could not focus on Nigel nor his arrogance, but I had to get things done. There were so many things that I had not said to my daddy that I felt that he needed to know, things that had really hurt me and had hurt my mom, brother, and sister. He had hurt my family, and we all had something that needed to be said, but we were out of time. So, I had to put together my father's goodbye from all the discussions that we had in the weeks before he passed. I pulled together what I felt my father would say to all of his family, friends, and some of his undetectable enemies.

Daddy's Goodbye

I was Leroy, Daddy, Grandpa, Bay Bro, Jealous Eye, and even Bro.
You all knew me and loved me for what you knew of me.

But did you really, really know me?
Did you know that I said I'm so sorry, Barbara?
Did you know that I cherished my children's accomplishments?
For they were my dreams realized!
Did you know my grandbabies were all my little super stars?
And that J Lee was my main man?
Did you know that my family: my sisters, brothers,
nieces and nephew, they made me proud?
They made me laugh and sometimes, they made me cry.
Did you know that I was sharp as a tack and as clean as a whistle?
Because it was what I knew, and it gave me something
that made me stand out amongst the crowd!
Did you that I was a friend, a neighbor and, oh yes,
your Brother and I gave you the best of me?

Now in saying goodbye,
I want you to live and live on,
for the best in each and every one of you is still yet to come!

My father was buried, and as he promised me, he found a way to help me pay off my debt with what he left me. I could not remember my father ever giving me anything without asking for it back, but this time there was no payment due. Paid in full!

Chapter IX

Death Comes Knocking at My Door

I had been burning the candle on both ends, non-stop! I had something to prove to everyone, the people at work, my staff, and, I guess, to myself. Once, I was near the end my evaluation came from my supervisor from the CDC, and it was awful. I exploded on my boss; he had never been there to observe all the work I had done for the Jefferson County Department of Health, yet he wanted to give me an average evaluation after all the shit that I had been through at the JCDH. I was so angry with my supervisor, and I told him; I immediately hung up and began to write my rebuttal, but I was hurting so very badly.

I went to get my son, and after we got home, I fed my son, and my head was pounding. I went into the bathroom and took two Aleve, and then I called my friend; he was a friend with benefits. I felt like that was what I needed, just someone to make me feel better. I put Jay to bed, and then my friend came over, and we spent a short amount of time together. He went into the bathroom, and all I was thinking was I should not have asked him over, and I was going to ask him to leave once he came out of the bathroom. As the door opened, he looked at me so strangely, and I was saying that he should leave, and he was saying, "What are you saying, Bridget? What are you saying," and I tried to say, "What is going on?" He said, "I got to get you to the hospital." He went and woke up Jay and all Jay wanted to do once he saw me was get a kiss, he said, "Mommy, you are salivating." My friend used the time that my son spent with me to get the car. And all I can remember is that it was pouring down rain, and once I made it outside, the rain was hitting me so hard. I was in the car headed to the hospital and my friend said, "I don't know where I am going, Jay. Little man, we are going to have to stop." He saw two carloads of policeman, and he asked them, and they just said it's around the corner. That was all the directions that the gave him. He found the hospital, and he ran inside and came running out immediately with two nurses, and they helped me into the wheelchair. At that very moment, I reached for Jay's hand, and I looked at him for what seemed as though it would be the last time I would lay eyes on my precious baby, and I passed out. And do you all want to know something? I bet that Satan was having a celebration, because he thought that he had gotten me, and oh my goodness, if I could have thought I would have said that he was right. But the devil is a liar! Once my mother got to me and sister and brother and some of my angels from work and along with my cousins, they began to pray, and God saved me! He put the devil to shame.

I survived a terrible stroke but not without residual damage. I talked very slowly, I could not write normally, and my left-rear carotid artery was completely blocked. And the most damaging was my ability to walk. I was told that I would never walk again, not normally. He ordered the nurse to bring me a walker, and at that very moment, Satan was ecstatic about the news that he was just doing a dance in the corner and cheering, saying, "Yes, I got her out of my way," until he heard me, in a very small and gentle voice, say to my mother, "No, the devil, is a LIAR!" I told her to help me up, and I began to walk without any type of walker or cane; I walked slowly, but I was walking! I guess that is what they mean when they say that there is power, absolute power in the tongue! When I speak over a thing, it comes to pass. When I said, "No, I will walk," all that I had to do was stand and try, and God did the rest, and he has been doing that every day since. Some days are more difficult, and the pain is excruciating, but Praise, God, I am walking! You have to fight sometimes to prove to our God that you are willing and able to go all the way! It is not because of my physician, because as I told you all the doctors had given up on me, but God! You have to understand that I did not walk on my own, it was Jesus that walked with me through it all and never gave up on me. That is why I am sitting here telling you all about how good my God is to me, and I am nobody special to him; I am just another one of his children. It has been fifteen years, and everyday there has been something that was worse than the other one, but I kept on praying and thanking God for his grace and mercy, and he did not have to do it, but he keeps doing it for me. And I know that he will do the same thing for you. All you have got to do is ask him in prayer and have the faith of a mustard seed. As it is written in Matthew 17:20, "And he said to them, 'Because of the littleness of your faith, for truly I say to you, if you have faith the size of a mustard seed, you will say to this mountain, Move from here to there, and it will move, and nothing will be impossible to you.'" Sisters and brothers, you just need faith and it will change your life for good and for the better! This is what I kept dreaming would happen for me! But was it only a dream or a temporary delay? It just seemed as though the rain would not stop falling.

Rainy Day

Sometimes the clouds hang so low you can barely breathe,
because the rain is just pouring down all around you.
Sometimes you just want to take a walk outside, but you simply can't,
because it just seems that the rain will never, ever stop.
Sometimes you open your window for a breath of fresh air, but instead you
get the smell of rain falling, and it makes you sad, and you sleep and sleep,
hoping that the morning will bring you into a new day.
Sometimes you pray and pray, asking God to make the rain stop,
but it never does end, and then you hear a small, loving voice saying it's a
rainy day, because I'm washing all of your sadness and heartaches away.
Now I understand why there are rainy days.

Chapter X

There Was a Runaway Train That Came Plowing Through

As my body and mind tried to recuperate, I went back to work, because I felt like I had to return. I was not in any shape to return to a job where the people were critical of my every moment, but I did go back. But let me drop this nugget on you; I was having dreams over the years of a beautiful baby girl. I knew that I didn't have a little girl, but I could not stop the dreams. In the dream, we would start off walking, and then we would be running from this evil huge black spirit. Sometimes it would be a spirit, sometimes it would be a man dressed in black, and sometimes it would be a monster, but we would always be running, and I would tell my baby to hold on to Mommy's hand and don't let go, and then I would wake up. I never asked anybody about the dream, even though it occurred more often and became much more vivid. We were in a park with a lake in the center of it. That was all that I could remember, other than us running for our lives. But I digress again, sorry. Once I returned back to work, everyone was nice, and I found out that there were several people who had spouses that had strokes in the same month as me, and they all passed away. Some of the people there were cruel, with no limits to what they could do to you, so I stayed in my office far away from the people with piercing eyes who wanted to see into my soul and destroy me one piece at a time. One morning,

I was walking down the hall, and I saw a short guy in the hall, and he passed me and said good morning and kept walking. He was a handsome young man, but there was something strange about him; he barely ever said a word to me. It concerned me, but I was not capable of speaking, so I let go of that very thought. My only thought was that I might die one day soon, and my thoughts ran rapid due to me having complete blockage of my left cardiac artery. I just knew that I had to have someone to take care of me and my son; I overlooked the obvious. And Satan saw me, and he must have sat back into his gigantic chair and smoked him a huge cigar and said, "Let the games begin."

My life with Chase was wonderful for the first three months; we went out and had such a nice time. I never suspected anything was wrong with Chase; he was such a gentleman. My first mistake again, letting him know what pleased me in a man. I always complimented him on how he was always so courteous, and then he really poured it on. And then, all of a sudden, people were talking about us, how I was too old for Chase, and that I was using him for sex. I could barely speak; me using anyone for sex? I was furious. The nerve of the people that I worked with was clearly off the chain. I wanted to just scream at them all; Chase looked much older, and I looked much younger. We had never asked each other's age, and everyone had some tea to spill concerning Chase and I's love life, WTF! I remained cool, and what happened next shocked me; Chase asked me to marry him, and I said yes. But a couple of weeks later, I found out that I was pregnant. I told Chase, and we got married at the courthouse immediately. It was like I went back into time and watched my mother's life suddenly become my life instantaneously. I could not wake myself up!

Chase turned on me like he did not know me; some days he was a nice guy, and other days he behaved like a monster that I could not recognize. We argued so much that he left me when I was about three months pregnant, and I begged him to come back, but instead of things getting better, they only got worst. The doctors told me that my baby was going to have severe birth defects, and I would be providing her with care for life and it would be best to abort. My favorite terms were, "the devil is a liar," "God gave this baby to me," and "I am going to keep my baby." It seemed like Chase really lost his mind; he became so jealous. He was so angry that one of my guy friends came to the job to visit me that he told me one day that we were going out to lunch, instead he got me in the car and all hell broke loose. He was driving like a maniac and pulling into parking spaces quickly and slamming on the brakes. I was holding to my stomach in an attempt to protect my baby. He did not stop until I told him I would never see the guy again. The guy was like a younger brother. Chase became obsessed with me, and it was so scary. My son was afraid of him; he took my little boy to football practice, and when Jay told him he did not want to play, he drug him off the field kicking and screaming. My baby came into the house with tears rolling down his face. He was terrified of Chase and his behavior.

It was finally time for my baby to come, and I was so ready. My Pumpkin had stayed too long, and I could just imagine why; she was probably saying, "Oh no, not me, I'm not going out there." It was so bad that Chase and I had an argument about a major blow out about where he was going to park at the hospital; this was on my delivery date. I had a Caesarian section, because my baby girl just refused to come out. It was probably because her mother was a nervous wreck. I broke down and began to cry in the room once they asked me to undress. The nurse asked me was I in pain, and I told her what happened, and she said sometimes our husbands just don't understand, and we have to just give them a pass on their immature behavior. She came back with something to calm me down, and all I can remember was my doctor saying it was time for her to leave, but she left me in the hands of an inexperienced resident who performed a C-section on me, and my baby was born just beautiful as God intended, but I was torn apart. I had been cut in the wrong direction and had staples. My recovery time was horrible, and I was sick as a I could be. Chase's mother came, and it seemed like she was going to be a great help to me, but that all fell apart. I had to do it all alone, with the exception of my sister coming and taking Bre' to her appointments. I was on my own, and Chase often reminded me of how I had chased his mother away, but I did not. I just wanted to hold my baby and that was what I asked her, to bring my baby, and she got so angry with me that she told me that she felt that I did not need her, and she left my house. Chase would not let that go, and he saw how much pain that I was in, and he would start an argument. This went on until I went back to work, and it just kept getting worse and worse, and finally, it broke. Chase had gotten laid off from work, and it was up to me to carry all the bills, and I needed to go to the bank, but Chase insisted that he would take me, so

I agreed, knowing that I had a separate account for an emergency for the baby. I just wrote the account number, and this bank teller asked me so many questions that had never been asked before that it made Chase suspicious, and he found out that I had a secret account, and that I had the statements going to my mother's house. I felt like Chase would ask me for the money, and it was all there for Bre's daycare in cases, such as the one we were in, with him being laid off from work again. Chase raised holy hell; he told me that he could not trust me and that I was a liar, and I tried to explain it to him that there was only nine hundred dollars in the account, but he persisted and called me a bitch. The next morning this went on, and he told me as I was walking out the door with my baby in my arms, he said, I" am going to kill your black ass!" I remember walking and getting into my car with tears streaming down my face and making it to the babysitter and just losing it. That was the beginning of the end for Chase and me; I could not do it anymore. I could just hear Satan laughing hysterically, because in that moment he had me. But God! There is always a ram in the bush. Just look at God when he provided a ram for Abraham in Genesis 22: 13, "Abraham looked up and there in a thicket he saw a ram caught by its horns. He went over and took the ram and sacrificed it as a burnt offering instead of his son." See, whenever you are down, and you feel as though you can't go on just lift your eyes to the Lord and trust that he has already made a way for you. Psalms 30:5 says, "Weeping may endureth for a night but joy cometh in the morning."

After all this, our marriage was destroyed. I went forward reluctantly to obtain my divorce. I felt like I had done something wrong, his mother and cousin were against me. I had not done anything to Chase but tried to help him. I helped him with the application for the job that he had gotten during our marriage, but no one remembered all they had was anger towards me. My family stayed out of this argument, but I was so glad that the Lord said vengeance is his, and I did not need family or friends. Because going through the process was one of the worst times in my life; the man that I had once loved turned his back to me. He even told me that he did not love me anymore. I could just hear the enemy laughing and saying, "You are the biggest fool on this planet to think that you had won the heart of this young brother, this is actually hilarious!" I would spend my nights in tears, because Chase and his mother were trying to take my baby away from me. They were basing it all on the stroke that I had which had damaged my memory, my thought process, and the way in which spoke. I said it once and I will say it again, but God! My God is an absolutely great God; the judge told Chase, "If the CDC believes in her ability to do her job, then I believe that she can care for her baby," and the judge let my baby stay with me. You see, when it is the darkest hour and you can't see your way out, all you have to do is call on the name of Jesus! And he will take total control of any and all situations; he did it for me, and I know that he will do the same for you, if not greater. And he will send the enemy back into the darkness with his head hung low, because our God demonstrates his power over the devil on a daily basis. If you can resist the devil, then he will flee as it is said in James 4:7. I could have tried to fight, but instead I stood still and let my God take control, and Satan took flight, and I won again!

Although I knew that I had won, I still was humiliated, because I could hear people all around me whispering and gossiping about me, and my family wasn't in the corner helping me to fight my way back. Chase treated me like I was a stranger. Once he had me pick up my daughter at a service station in an undesirable neighborhood. When I pulled up, he got out of the car and handed me my daughter; he never spoke to me or acknowledged that I was there. He went on to put her bag and car seat in the car, and he got back in his car and sped away, leaving me standing in dismay. As I stood there with prostitutes, drug addicts, and drunkards around, attempting to calm my baby girl down while I got her car seat in, and I began to cry, and then all of a sudden, I felt a calming come over my body ,and it seemed like the parking lot that once was filled seemed as though it was empty. I was now able get the car seat in, and my baby I placed in the seat and gave her a cup with apple juice, and we were driving off. The only way I can explain what happened was as if the angel of God took control of that environment and me, to help me feel calm, until I got everything settled. You see, I have always prayed that Jesus would put an umbrella of protection around me wherever I go. And that was what Jesus did for me in that very instance, and if he can do that for me, surely he can do that same thing for you, no matter how large or small your situation may be; God is always with you. He is just waiting on you to talk with him. I was so tired and feeling so alone in that instance I thought I should RUN away from the pain, agony, and heartache. I was going through this alone, and I decided at that moment that I would Run! So, I ran, but I could not run for long because of my baby. Bre' was born with one chromosome out of order, and it caused her bones to be soft, her legs bow, and she was determined that she was not meant to be in braces for life. She continuously ran right out of them every week, and we had to go and get them repaired so much that everyone in the office knew my little one's name. "Hi, Bre'," is what they would say to her, and she would reply with the biggest smile, "Hello!" So, me being worn completely out, going to Atlanta was a welcomed break. Although I hated the idea of moving to a city filled with people everywhere and traffic for days, I knew that there were physicians there that were going to make my daughter better. When I met with the doctor, and he told me that he could absolutely fix Bre's legs, I hugged him so tight with tears streaming down my face; it was one of the best days of my life. I knew that I would be at peace for once and all, because things were starting to turn around. In Psalms 27:14 it says, "wait on the Lord: be of good courage, and he shall strengthen thine heart: wait I say, on the LORD."

Chapter XI

The Sound of the Mother Land, Africa is A-Calling

Mask Man

Mask man, hiding his true identity.
Mask man, who only wants to deceive and manipulate.
Mask man, cheating and lying from the very start.
Mask man, a seduction artist, deceiving the one who loves him most.
Mask man, so full of jealousy and anger,
all hidden behind a beautiful smile in those radiant, light brown eyes
Mask man, mask removed to reveal the little child filled with pain that whom
the devil has captured never to be released to society again

Once I settled down in Atlanta, I moved to Gwinnett County. The people at my job said that I had moved to one of the wealthiest counties in Georgia, but I was so far from being wealthy or even next door to it. So, this is how I got to move to the suburbs of Gwinnett. I was praying and telling God that I was okay where I was staying, and he said NO! I told him that I had looked and looked and there was nothing. He told me to take one more look, and I did; it was like out of nowhere that the house had appeared, and he told me to set up an appointment. I loved it, my kids loved it, and within a matter of two weeks, we were in a new place. The thing that I have to tell you all is just listen to God. He is that still, gentle voice that you hear when the world is calm all around you and you are calm on the inside, and he will talk with you. God is with us all the time but we are in a world of chaotic situations on a daily basis so we cannot hear him. In order that we may hear from God we must pray. In Matthew 18:19-20 it says, "Again I say to you, that if two of you agree on earth about anything they ask, it will be done for them by My Father who is in heaven. For where two or three are assembled in My name, there I am in their midst."

As we got settled in, it became more and more apparent that we needed a church. I began to ask people wherever I went; I was simply determined to find us a church home. My determination payed off; my daughter and I went into this beautiful, adorable little bakery, and it was owned by a beautiful sister, and they had the best caramel cake, but what she told me about her church I had to go and experience it for myself. Grace Family International Church was an African church that I fell in love with, because for the first time, I felt like I was at home. They worshipped differently; they called upon the Lord, wiith brothers and sisters with serious anointing over their lives. I was finally home. There was one woman that was a prophet that had come to Grace Family, and she spoke with me last, just as the service was ending, and she told me that I had been speaking to the Lord about a lot of things, and that he had heard me, and that my prayers were soon to come true. I thought okay. And then I forgot about it, because this woman didn't say anything specific, she just generalized, and in the word, it states in Matthew 7:15, "Beware of the false prophets, which come to you in sheep's clothing, but inwardly they are ravening wolves." I don't know whether she was or not, but I do remember this experience. My mother says this from time to time, be careful who you let pray over you and prophesize over your life. She says this all the time, I can pray over my own pains.

I participated in everything that they had, and it was wonderful. Then I met a tall handsome guy, and he was like my dream come true, and I shared my thoughts with the first lady of the church, and she told me that he was married. That tore my heart right from my chest; I was devastated. He told me that his wife was in Nigeria, and she never would come to see him. At first,

I said no, we can't see each other, but my son took to him, and before we knew it, we were friends. In the meantime, I had met a man through Facebook, his name was Sasung. He was a nice guy, but I was happy with my friend. He asked me a lot of questions about the man I called friend, and I shared the information with him never, ever thinking anything of it. But low and behold, Sasung had gone and prayed about my friend, and he told me that he was married, that he had children, and that he was never going to get a divorce from his wife. I could not believe it, and he told me to ask him and to tell him where this information had come from, so I did. And just as he said it was all true, I cried over it. I did not speak to Sasung for about a couple of weeks. Then he wrote me asking me was it true. And my answer was yes. Then he told me that a very close male family relative was going to be diagnosed with cancer, but he was going to be okay. I found out that my uncle had cancer, and I told my mom that my friend had seen it before we knew about it and that my uncle was going to be just fine. These things, as well as some other things that he had done or told me to do for my children, I did, and they made me closer than ever to him. I was falling in love with him, and I was blinded by the woods that he had raised up all around me. Sasung wanted me trapped and confused as he was. "But if our gospel is hidden, it is hidden to those who are lost. The god of this world has blinded the minds of those who do not believe, lest the light of the glorious gospel of Christ, who is the image of God, should shine on them." But don't you dare give up on my God, not yet, not ever! "God is **Faithful,** by whom ye were called unto the fellowship of his Son Jesus Christ our Lord." (1 Corinthians 1:9) Trust me, he never left my side. As with you, he will never leave you, even in the moments of total distress.

As I continued to walk with God, I suddenly stopped listening to God's word completely because of my own wants and desires; I began to fall. Now, I had Sasung in one ear whispering all the sweet things that I wanted to hear, that I needed to know, and there was God in the other ear telling me to put a pause on Sasung but did I? NO! I kept pushing it forward. Sasung asked me to marry him as soon as he knew that he had captured my full attention. He started to Skype me and spend all of his free time with me. I was still telling him no, because I did not want to marry him, because he was ten years younger than myself. But he would not stop pressuring me. I finally told him that I would come to Africa, and if I felt something when he held my hand, then I would marry him. He was so certain that I would that he took my dress size, and he was so certain that nothing was going to prevent us from getting married. Everyone was against me going to Nigeria, but my mind was made up and all I wanted was to be in his presence. There was news that some men had kidnapped some girls in Nigeria, and the world was in an uproar. But I could not be stopped; God was trying to get my attention, but I had closed my eyes to everything except the love that Sasung was displaying. The night that I went, there was a terrible storm, and I missed my connecting flight and had to spend the night all alone at the airport gate, awaiting the plane's departure, never once did I think to pray to God after this unusual hang up with me missing my flight. The next morning there was a missionary and her children going over to meet her husband, and she came over to me while holding her infant child, asking where I was going. I answered her saying Ibadan, Nigeria. She asked was I alone, and I told her I was, but I was going to meet a friend, and she asked if I had ever been to Nigeria, and I had to tell her no. She smiled at me and said in the sweetest voice, "Is this a man from Ibadan that you met here?" and I said no again. Then, all of a sudden, the airplane was about to board, and she said, "May we pray for you?" and I said yes. She called her other three children around me, and they began to pray for me. She hugged me so tight, and she said to me, "You are covered with the blood of Jesus." She boarded the plane first, and after we landed, I never saw her again.

Once my plane landed in Lagos, Nigeria my heart was beating a hundred miles per hour. I was going to see him, and I could not breathe. I could not find him, and I asked a man for his phone, and I called him, and he was standing right in front of my eyes. He was a very handsome man, and he was smiling so big, and his eyes would have captured any woman's attention. He was beautiful inside and out, and he reached for my hand, and I put my hand into his hand, and I knew that I was his and he was mine, so I thought. He brought me a huge, fake flower, and of course, I said thank you, but clearly, I was so shocked and wanted to laugh, but he was trying for me. He had a taxi waiting for us, and when we got into the car, he reached over to give me a very nice kiss. He was a gentleman, just what I had told him what was missing in my previous relationships. The taxi driver began to drive, and he just pulled right out into traffic and scared me so badly that I grabbed Sasung's hand and screeched a little. I whispered to Sasung, "Where is the seatbelt?" and he looked at me totally perplexed. "There aren't any." He smiled at me and held me close. We spent the night together at the hotel, and he was a gentleman all night; never tried anything. He was perfect!

The next day was the day he had planned for our wedding day, May 29th. I had told him that I would know, and we had both agreed that we were ready. He and I got dressed in these amazing red and white African garments. My braids were wrapped in a gorgeous red head wrap; I had a woman to come and help me get dressed. It was like something I had only dreamt of, and this was all happening, because Sasung had asked me to marry him, and I said yes. We left in a caravan with an armed policeman in a car in front of us and one in back of us, so I was told. We traveled to another town that was at least two hours away from Ibadan. We passed through villages where there were one room huts, and I saw so many of the black people that I had dreamed of my whole life. They were here in Africa and so was I; I was so excited. I had the man that I loved, and he was constantly staring into my eyes. I kind of felt like okay, this is strange, but what the hell; we will go with it! Can you imagine Satan sitting there? He's got popcorn popping; it is running over from the popcorn machine onto the floor as he is takes one big handful after another and just gulps it down while laughing at me and his evil little minions all around him jumping and pointing at me as they have taken control of Sasung. And he is forced to do exactly as the puppeteer demands of him. And I am the biggest joke of the day! So they think!

We arrived at this magnificent building, and I was instantly transported back into time. The alleys were all damaged buildings that looked like they had been there since Christ walked upon the land, and we were walking through on a road paved with stones. And we were on the outside of this huge building that looked as though it had suffered numerous attacks. We were in a room filled with people that I didn't know, but who were playing a role in my marriage. It was so strange, and we were married by some crazy-looking man of God that was only interested in the handful of money that Sasung had brought him. And again, I thought this was some weird-ass shit, but again Sasung came over to me, staring into my eyes, and I was like, "Okay, let's go with it!" And I was married to my African King!

After the wedding, we took pictures, and Sasung's brother, who was assigned to watch over me, was now working my last nerve by constantly wiping my face, clearing it of sweat. It was so hot that I knew I had melted. Get this. The entire wedding party had on long sleeves, and not one of them were sweating. I called my mother and told her that every person I saw there was black, but I was the negro sweating. I know Sasung's brother must have wiped my face at least fifty times during my stay. We drove back, had a big meal, and went back to the hotel where Sasung could not wait to consummate the marriage. During the process, some really weird shit happened. It was like he blew into my nose during intercourse, and he did not stop until it was over. I asked him about his behavior, and he laughed and said that was something that they did in Africa to make the couple's relationship grow stronger. During my stay in Nigeria, I met his family, friends, and colleagues. We did things for his very first time, like going to the movies, which we did that twice in a row, because he really like it. We ate at American restaurants, and we went to the zoo, which was so interesting, because there were so few animals for it to be Africa. We took some fabulous pictures, and I never, ever knew that this was all a part of his personal agenda. He was told by the photographer that the pictures would be ready, but he was a couple of days behind, and Sasung went to his office, and he asked the guy about them, speaking in his dialect, and all of a sudden, he slapped the man down to his knees. I should have known right then that Sasung was going to be abusive to me, but I was so in love, just as Sasung had planned me to be. There was even a woman threatening to have Sasung arrested, and foolish me, I saved him and ignored all of this outrageous behavior. Never realizing that it was God giving me signs, and I was too blind to see what I was walking into. Before I left Nigeria, I met Sasung's mother who was deathly ill; she could not rise from the sofa. She could not open her eyes, nor could she speak. I felt terrible for her, and on the flight home, I prayed for her and Sasung's family. He seemed to be of the upper class, but he was actually living below the poverty line. That is why you cannot judge a book by its cover. I wanted to help Sasung and his family live healthier and better lives; I knew that God had called on me to help these people, and I was more than thrilled to do it. I was saving the man of my dreams and making the worst mistake of my life.

On my ride to the airport, Sasung put that pain down on the inside of me; he cried with me and sent me a picture of himself crying, telling me he was going to miss me, and we cried together. On the flight home, my heart was so heavy; all I could think of was Sasung and his mother. As soon as I got home, I went to Western Union and sent Sasung and his mother a substantial amount of money. I begin to work on Sasung's application both day and night. I stayed on the phone with the immigrations officer, and I stayed in prayer. I prayed and prayed for Sasung to come to America. While I was praying, Sasung was doing everything like a single man could do. It became so bad that I began to ask my male friends and colleagues if I should send for this man who I felt was cheating on me. They told me that it would all stop once he came to America. They assured me, and I told Sasung about my fears, and he said I was just feeling sad, because we had not been together, and everything would be wonderful once he got here, and that there was something that he had to destroy once he got here. He asked if I trusted him, and I said yes. The morning of his interview, I felt like I was called to pray, and I went downstairs, and I felt that Satan was sitting on my sofa, looking at me. I could see him in a black suit smoking a cigar and laughing. Right then, I began to pray for Sasung, never knowing what was planned for my life. Even Sasung told me that he had been told by God that he would come to America on behalf of a woman, and I would not stop him. And Satan saw all of this, and he saw me wanting to help Sasung and his family, me wanting to bring them all over here. I had a house big enough for them all, and I wanted to help Sasung and his entire family, and I believed that was what God was telling me to do. It was not until I saw Sasung walk through those doors at the Atlanta airport that it finally hit me that something had gone terribly wrong. As Sasung walked through those doors at the airport, it was like someone had put me in a hypnotic state; it was like everything stopped moving in the airport except Sasung and I. As I watched this thin, frail, dirty, black man that I did not know walk slowly past me, there was something on the inside of him that looked like an evil minion of the devil, and it was looking at me as Sasung continued to walk towards me, and all of a sudden, my baby grabbed my hand and said, "Mommy, are you okay?" And the atmosphere around me was unfrozen, and there was movement again. And I looked down at my baby's eyes and said, "Yes, baby, I am okay." Sasung walked over to me and hugged me. And I said it silently right then, "OMG, what have I done?" The thing that I had forgotten was God is in control! You see, no matter how bad a situation may seem, God is in control! So, don't give up, just begin to pray and ask God for his mercy, and grace, and plead the blood of Jesus over yourself and your household. Stand strong in faith and never let fear destroy you from reaching your destiny. Psalm 34:4 says, "I sought the Lord, and he answered me, and delivered me from all my fears." This is why I am telling you that you must pray; pray like your life depends on it, because God answers desperate, heartfelt prayers, my brothers and sisters.

As Sasung and I began our life together, the arguments began soon afterwards. You see, Corinthians 6:14 says, "do not be yoked together with unbelievers." We could not live together in peace; we argued every day. Sasung even said he wanted to go home. And I asked that he give it some more time. You see, I still failed to see that Sasung had brought the enemy with him from Africa. He was doing some evil things to me in our bedroom that he had started in Nigeria; he would constantly breathe in my nose. But God was with me, he never left me, even though I had been disobedient to him. I had a vivid dream one night; there were three old Indian women, and they said, "Tell Sasung to go, and we will leave." I woke up and told Sasung, and he told me that I needed to pray. I got up in went into my prayer room and began to pray out loud like I have been doing, and Sasung told me to pray in silence, and I looked at him, bewildered that he said that to me, being that he was supposed to be a man of great faith. I told him no, I was going to continue to pray aloud for the Lord has answered too many of my prayers to pray silently. He would not leave; instead, he became more and more evil. He tried to kill me, and he slammed me down on the bed, and then he said, "What if I killed you right now? Who would know?" and I said, "Our neighbors, my family, and my baby." As I tried to get up, he slammed me down on the bed and pulled down his pants and forced himself inside of me and raped me. With tears rolling down my face, I could not say a word. He had his hand around my neck, and once he was done, he let go of me and left the house. I called his family and told them of his behavior, and they knew about it and never opened their mouth to say a word to me. It was not their fault nor their responsibility to tell me anything, but it was mine, because I have a relationship with Jesus where he allows his holy spirit to tell me everything, but it was on me for acting out of disobedience when I had been shown that Sasung was not the man for me. There was another time when Sasung totally ignored a situation. He told me that he owed a man in Lagos a large sum of money. The police came to his mother's house, and when they could not find Sasung, they took his mother into custody. She was in jail for about two to three days. Sasung stopped talking; we did not have any money to get her out. Somehow, they got the money, and she was released but at a terrible cost. She was raped while she was incarcerated. She would not speak for months, and Sasung refused to talk about it; he started to stay out all times of night, saying that he was working, but I knew that he was cheating on me.

I was praying so much that God started to show up all around me; there was one morning that I got up early in the morning and went out to sit on the patio with a cup of coffee, and as I was starting to sit, I saw the face of Jesus, and I heard Sasung, and I called for him to make sure I was not going crazy, and I asked him what did he see, and he said the face of Jesus, and he turned and walked away, but I could not. For it was the most beautiful thing I had ever seen in my life. There were so many things going wrong; my boss was putting me under so much pressure, and I was so absolutely stressed out that I almost loss my vision. I had to have surgery done, and you won't believe what happened. The woman at the registration desk knew Sasung; she pulled me to the back and told me that he had brought a woman in, and he called her his aunt. When I confronted him about it, he denied it and said that woman could not remember him, and she had told me that she knew it was him because of his accent, and she said he told her he was from Africa. Sasung was cheating on me, nearly caused me to lose my mind! I just had completely fallen down, and I was unable to speak. And Satan was standing up and applauding saying, "Bravo! Bravo, my evil little minion! Bravo!" But God! I am telling you "when God is for you, who DARE be against you," as is stated in Romans 8:31. Sasung was showing me very little sympathy as everything started to crash and burn all around me; I had a severe panic attack on my job and was hospitalized. I was so anxious about going to staff meetings that I would become nervous and have headaches before they started. I would have episodes of vertigo, where the dizziness was so terrible that I would vomit all over the floor, and this was not me. I was confident and charismatic and vocal during staff meetings. I was down, so lost, and I could not find my way. I went to a therapist and was diagnosed with severe depression. I could not stop crying, and the therapist said no more work! And I had to leave Georgia, and we were on our way to Alabama. I had left home, and now I was on my way back to a place that I should have known as home, but it always felt as though I was a tourist on my worst vacation. I just did not know how bad things were going to get. But I was sure going to find out.

Sasung was so ready to leave Georgia; we did not have any help except for Jay's friend who lived across the street from us. Sasung prepared goat for dinner, and we sat and laughed and talked, and I said it will be good to get a fresh start. Sasung and I were going to be the better for it. And he looked at me totally confused, and said, "You mean Sasung is going to be moving with you?" I said, "Of course, he is my husband; where would he be going?" Sasung had gotten up and pretended to be washing the dishes. The guy said, "Well, I guess I will be going; I will see you guys before you leave." I turned to Sasung and said, "What was that all about?" and he said, "What?" And I told him what the guy had said, and he said, "You know these young people, they think what they want." It is just so amazing what God brings back to your remembrance. The next morning, we were off, and we arrived at my mother's house, and about a day after we had arrived, my mother had so many rules that we could not abide by that we had to leave to go to my sister's house. We began right away trying to get Sasung a job working in his field as a nurse's aid, and he was working in no time flat. He worked the evening shift and came home all the time, but soon things started to change. He stopped calling me and started to come home much later, stating that he had to take his friend home. He started to work every day, and we began to argue about the smallest things. I was doing all that I could to keep the peace in the home, washing the clothes, cooking meals, and even cleaning up. But Sasung and I were arguing so much that it made my sister and her family uncomfortable. So, I told Sasung it was time for us to go, and I prayed about it, and we found a small town house close to Monica, because I was still sick and had problems with my memory and would have to go to my sister's house due to me having a bad episode with vertigo. Things got really bad once we moved into our townhouse. Sasung stayed at work and would not come home until in the morning. I told my sister about it, and she said just call him at work, so I did, and a woman answered the phone like she was just shocked to hear my voice, and she asked, "Who are you?" And I was just stunned, and I said, "I am Sasung's wife," and she said, "Hold on," and Sasung answered the phone like someone was standing over him, and I told him that I needed a ginger ale and some Pepto Bismol, because I had an upset stomach. He said okay, and then he asked why I didn't call him on his phone, and I said, because you stopped returning my calls until he was on his way home. He said okay, and I told him that I really needed the medicine. When he got home, he was furious, but he tried to hide it. He told me that he was going to sleep in the other room, because he did not want to disturb me. He got up early that next morning and left for work. But it was too late; God had seen my tears and heard me calling on him. You know people used to always tell me, if you don't want an answer please don't pray for one, because our father will definitely give you one. As it is stated in Romans 8:28, "And we know that in all things God works for the good of those who love him, who have been called according to his purpose." So, my unanswered prayers were heard all through the atmosphere, and God had only just begun to give me answers to my prayers. You see, when something or someone did to disturb your spirit, all you have to do is talk with God about it, and it will be done just that quick.

Things begin to happen right away, no hesitation, because pray was all I did all day long. First, I found a pair of Sasung's underwear that were hidden, and they were covered in bodily fluids from after you have had sex with someone and wiped yourself clean with them. Then there was a dream where I saw this young girl telling Sasung that she was pregnant, and that the child was his. When I told him about all that I had found and seen in a vison, he adamantly denied it all. He left our house one day going to the doctor's office and never came back home, I called his job and he wasn't there but in the next twenty minutes he was home. I asked him what had happened at the doctor's office, and he told me he wasn't telling me a got damn thing. That was it. I told him he had to go and to take his clothes with him; he jumped into his car and went to the police station and brought them to our townhouse and tried to get me arrested, but he could not. I do believe it was because I spoke calmly to the police officer and told her what had happened and that he came home immediately although I never spoke to him. The police sent him away, and he returned the next day. We argued again, and he went back to the police, and they came back and told him that they were not counselors, and they sent him away again. I prayed and prayed, and one morning, I dreamt a big yellow python came right down the middle of our bed between Sasung and I, and I was not afraid; I was done. That night Sasung came home and went into the other bedroom, and I told him that if he could not stand to sleep next to me, it was time for him to go, and he said, "Yes, it is time for me to go." He said, "I am tired of you and your whole family being in my life," and he packed his things, and while I was angry at him, it was the best move that he could have ever done for me. He did not call me for two weeks; he told my brother-in-law that he had moved in with a woman. My brother-in-law told him that he must have lost his mind. Sasung told him that he didn't have any place to go; my brother-in-law told him, "We don't do things like that here in America to our wives, unless we are planning not to come back home, I wish you the best, bruh. You are traveling down a road of no return."

Sasung called me back when he saw that things were not going to work out with this woman. He came to the townhouse but would not come near my front door, and I was wondering what the problem was. He told me that he was afraid of me, and I laughed and laughed at him. The reason that I laughed was because I knew that the devil was not afraid of me; he had done so many evil and foul things to me. I could not take a single word that he would say as truth, because he was a habitual liar. I had called him over to let him know that I had paid the rent for his mother's apartment for a year, and that I had spoken to his sister, and I had told her that I was going to take him back. It was like he didn't hear what I was saying, he wanted me to give him a thousand dollars, and that was all that he would talk about with me. So, I refused, and that made him angry as hell, but it wasn't because I wasn't going to give it to him, but he knew that he no longer could control me. He knew that I had begun to take my power back. He jumped into his car and just burnt the rubber completely off his tires, and all that I could see was the devil getting in that car on fire from his head to his toes, all ablaze from the inside, outward flaming as he took off in his vehicle from hell, leaving a trail of smoke and fire behind. I began to laugh as I turned and walked away, but my joyous mood was swallowed up by a note that I received on messenger, and this is the note with name of the author taken out to protect the one who did not know better. Note in its entirety:

"How are you just wanted to inform you of how your husband has been living with me for months we have been together for over two years now I'm am currently carrying his child that u couldn't have for him and we are together when you think he at work he with me building a family with me he has a recording in your house we sit and watch you I'm sure he with u now getting you to sign divorce papers he only married you for his green card an citizenship he never did love you so please stop texting and blowing up his phone he has been cheating on u for almost two years my name is - - I'm a nurse at his job that's how we meet ask him to tell u the truth as why he tells me u can't give him a baby so he doesn't want u or better yet ask him why he stop sleeping with you if u need anything else I'm available to talk

"Tell sasug I will see him when he gets home"

Yes, this was the letter sent to me with no punctuation and Sasung's name was even misspelled. This woman was foolish enough to believe that Sasung would really want to give up his major supply, me. He has not stop calling or texting me until this day. But you see, because of my religious belief, he is a Jezebel spirit, that is why I call him Satan. You see, this woman does not know that she means nothing to Sasung; she is only a means to an end and so is the child. I can't tell her, because he has filled her head with nothing but lies about me to only manipulate her to meet all of his needs. And this is what is called a narcissist, because he couldn't care less about destroying me only to get what he wants; the arrogance of him. That is why it is best that we go no contact with them, because they try to take total control over your mind, body, and soul. She told me what they had been doing, and it answered all of the questions that I had been asking him since before he came, and it was all in this one note from a deranged, pregnant mistress of a narcissistic man. I had told Sasung about the women here in America, and that he had to be aware of them and take all precautions. The enemy never, ever sends you something that you are not attracted to, but he will send you something that is so desirable, and you won't be able to pray the enemy away from you. And Sasung was not that man; he walked away from God. Do you know a man or woman that has been tested, and they failed it, and they lost everything? Sasung did not know he was being tested, nor did he take the time to look closely at the situation in which God led him into, and that caused him to fail God's test miserably.

After I cried all day and night, I knew about the baby, because God does not leave me in the dark pertaining to any type of relationship I am involved with in my life. He told me, but Sasung would not admit the truth, and Sasung told me that I was crazy, that I did not know anything. And Sasung is calling me and texting me up until this day, asking me to let him back in or to take me out to dinner, but most of the time I don't answer him unless it is pertaining to our business together. It is best to block a narcissistic man or woman out of your life, so they cannot communicate with you, because you need that time to heal and not to hear the lies, manipulations, and deceitful things that the narcissistic man has set up in his mind, a place to play you once again, but this time it will be much worst. I know this, because I put Sasung out of my house so many times, and I took him back because of those flying monkeys in his family; these are people that believe every word that he says. But every time I took him back, the next situation was worse than the one before. He would come home late, smelling like a woman's perfume. He would not tell me where he was, and he wouldn't let me touch his phone. And now I know that he is under a Jezebel spirit or in our psychological terminology, Narcissistic Personality Disorder. A narcissistic individual is a person who lacks empathy and thinks only of himself in the most grandiose manner, never thinking of anyone else's emotions or feelings and blaming others for his wrongdoing. This is why Sasung did these appalling things to me and became the monster; I never dreamt I would fall in love with someone like him. I was devastated and cried until it felt like my tears were made up of blood. Sasung promised me that he was not going to mishandle me like all the other men that were in my life, he promised that he would be faithful to me, and he promised that we would have a marriage that people would always be excited about and ask us how we do it.

I Surrender All to You

I surrender myself to you, even though it killed me on the inside
I surrender my whole being without any thought,
because you were my soulmate
I surrender myself when you wanted love from me continuously, non-stop
I surrender myself when you told me things that I found to be unbelievable
I surrender myself in hopes that I could somehow change you
if I just loved you enough
I surrender myself to a man that I had brought from another land
I surrender myself for all the things that I knew about my God
and trusted you when you said our beliefs were the same
I surrender myself to nothing more than a liar, deceiver and manipulator

I surrender myself to my God as the winds blow for the storm that I created Do you have a such a person in your life, a person that God never gave you permission to marry, with true narcissistic or Jezebel behavior? If so, please get out of that relationship and go no contact. Your life could depend on it.

Chapter XII

The Great Awakening

AWOKE!

I am awakening, no more clouds floating around
over my head every damn day!
I am awakening, and the rain will finally STOP!
I am awakening, I can see family and friends
for who they really are to me
I am awakening, I don't have to take your mistreatment
to survive another day
I am awakening, I won't let you abuse me
mentally, verbally, or physically ever again!
I am awakening, I don't need your attention,
or better yet, your money to prove to me that you love me,
when I know that you could care less about me
I am awakening, I can see that the one who carried me
through all of the storms and rain was none other than Jesus!
The great, I AM!
I am AWOKE! I don't ever have to take shit from you again!

I don't know who I am fully, not yet, but I do know that I am traveling down a road where there is joy, sunshine and peace. And me writing this book was God's way of helping me through this storm and to open up my eyes made me aware that I was empathic, understanding, and sharing the feelings of others. And I knew that the men in my life, and even my father, were narcissistic, never caring about another's feeling, with arrogant and grandiose behavior and doing foul and terrible things. In the spiritual world, this person is known as someone acting under the Jezebel spirit. This is someone who is plagued with demonic spirits. They are weak people who can be easily controlled by Satan. And he does take total control over their lives and makes them his little puppet. He is the master puppeteer, and he set out to destroy anyone that God has anointed with a purpose. So, you see, if God has given you a specific gift, the enemy will target you. Satan does not want children of God to ever reach their destiny, because he knows that we are just saving souls and bringing him closer to his traumatic ending, he knows it is coming. As it says in God's word in Revelation 20:7-10,

> And when the thousand years are expired, Satan shall be loosed out of his prison, And shall go out to deceive the nations which are in the four quarters of the earth, Gog and Magog, to gather them together to battle: the number of whom is as the sand of the sea. And they went up on the breadth of the earth, and compassed the camp of the saints about, and the beloved city: and fire came down from God out of heaven and devoured them. And the devil that deceived them was cast into the lake of fire and brimstone, where the beast and the false prophet are, and shall be tormented day and night for ever and ever.

You see, Satan is counting on all of his evil demonic minions to take control and to destroy millions of you who God has summoned to be warriors. We have all been called upon to save souls. And so, God gave us his word as our sword and the ability to pray, and as it is states in Ephesians 6:10-19,

Finally, my brethren, be strong in the Lord, and in the power of his might. Put on the whole armor of God, that ye may be able to stand against the wiles of the devil. For we wrestle not against flesh and blood, but against principalities, against powers, against the rulers of the darkness of this world, against spiritual wickedness in high places. Wherefore take into you the whole armor of God, that ye may be able to withstand in the evil day, and having done all, to stand. Stand therefore, having your loins girt about with truth, and having on the breastplate of righteousness; And your feet shod with the preparation of the gospel of peace; Above all, taking the shield of faith, wherewith ye shall be able to quench all the fiery darts of the wicked. And take the helmet of salvation, and the sword of the Spirit, which is the word of God: Praying always with all prayer and supplication in the Spirit and watching thereunto with all perseverance and supplication for all saints. And for me, that utterance may be given unto me, that I may open my mouth boldly, to make known the mystery of the gospel.

You see, our father was not just thinking of one of us but all of us. It is time for you all to wake up and hear the voice of our Lord, he is waiting. But know this, he can't wait very much longer. He has given each of you free will to decide your fate; let it be with our father, Jesus. Use your talents, skills, and abilities to assist others. Now is the time for all of us to use our God-given task to help others see how wonderful it is to serve God. I am going to close with these Four Things in which Minister Kevin L. A. Ewing said you would need to be saved.

Repentance: Repent of all of your sin, ask for God forgiveness and you will be saved. 2 Chronicles 7:14, "If my people, which are called by my name, shall humble themselves and pray, and seek my face, and turn from their wicked ways; then will I hear from heaven, and will forgive their sin, and will heal their land."

Forgive: Forgiveness is not for the person that wrong you, but it is for you and your healing process. Numbers 14:18, "The Lord is long-suffering, and of great mercy, forgiving iniquity and transgression, and by no means clearing the guilty, visiting the iniquity of the fathers upon the children and unto the third and fourth generation."

Follow God's Commandments: Follow the commandments of our father, for they will help you live a more righteous life. **Exodus 20: 3-17, "Thou shalt have no other gods before me. Thou shalt not make unto thee any graven image, or any likeness of any thing that is in heaven above, or that is in the earth beneath, or that is in the water under the earth: Thou shalt not bow down thyself to them, nor serve them: for I the Lord thy God am a jealous God, visiting the iniquity of the fathers upon the children unto the third and fourth generation of them that hate me; And shewing mercy unto thousands of them that love me, and keep my commandments. Thou shalt not take the name of the Lord thy God in vain; for the Lord will not hold him guiltless that taketh his name in vain. Remember the sabbath day, to keep it holy. Six days shalt thou labour, and do all thy work: But the seventh day is the sabbath of the Lord thy God: in it thou shalt not do any work, thou, nor thy son, nor thy daughter, thy manservant, nor the maidservant, nor thy cattle, nor thy stranger that is within thy gates: For in six days the lord made heaven and earth, the sea, and all that in them is, and rested the seventh day: wherefore the Lord blessed the sabbath day, and hallowed it. Honor thy father and thy mother: that thy days may be long upon the land which the Lord thy God giveth thee. Thou shalt not kill. Thou shalt not commit adultery. Thou shalt not steal. Thou shalt not bear false witness against thy neighbor. Thou shalt not covet thy neighbor's house, thou shalt not covet thy neighbor's wife, nor his manservant, nor his maidservant, nor his ox, nor his ass, nor any thing that is thy neighbor's."**

Do not speak negativity: You should never speak over someone life negatively. Death and life are in the power of the tongue: and they that love it shall eat the fruit thereof. Proverbs 18:21

Realize this, my brothers and sisters, now that you are woke, Satan is going to call up all hell against you. He must try to win. Just take a look at my life, since I stopped and took a sincere look around. Satan stood up and called all his demons, IDOTS! He said to every witch, warlock, demon, and evil spirit, "I will have to do it myself!" He stood up in hell and stomped his cigar out as his whole entire body was sat a blaze and said, "I COMMAND ALL OF HELL TO COME AGAINST RENEE' AND BRE' AND DO NOT STOP UNTIL THEY ARE BROKEN AND SHAME HAS TAKEN TOTAL CONTROL FOR GOOD!" AND HE LAUGHED AND LAUGHED AS HE PULLED OUT HIS FLAMING SWORD AND WHIRLED IT UP, AND A WIND BLEW UP EVERY EVIL DEMONIC THING IN HELL! AND HE LAUGHED SO LOUD THAT IT SOUNDED LIKE A TORNADO FROM HELL BENEATH US. But he does not know the God that I serve! My God is great, almighty, and never, ever fails! I began to pray, calling upon my God to break all generational curses, to defeat my enemies, burning down every evil altar that had been erected with my name on it, defeating every witch and warlock, breaking every contract that had been signed without my knowledge, and burning any and every enemy up from the inside out, leaving him in nothing but ashes which the ANGELS FROM HEAVEN would blow with their mighty breath, and it would take those ashes to the north, south, east, and west, never to return together again. I declared it and decreed it, and it was done! In the MIGHTY NAME OF JESUS! AMEN, AMEN, AND AMEN! This is the way we can win; KEEP YOUR EYES ON GOD!

Conclusion

I was spoken to by God and asked to write this book. God gave me through so many experiences. Everywhere I turned I heard him speaking to me and being insistent about me finishing this book, but I felt like I couldn't, because I did not have an ending, and I was afraid to put such personal information in a book, but God reminded me that this was for his people to be saved. And immediately my thoughts returned to Sasung; it made sense. Sasung was the man that I thought would be in my life forever, but something was amiss about Sasung's personality and that caused our relationship to all fall apart. I began looking for answers, and they all pointed to a Jezebel spirit. And all the YouTube channels kept declaring to me that I was a survivor of narcissistic abuse. Everything had happened in my life according to God's plan. It was all a part of the **PROCESS** to bring me to this place where I am at this very moment. You see, God does not give you skills, talents, or abilities for no reason; he means for them to be used. And you will use them no matter what your procedure may be to get it done. Mine was one of pain and disappointment, but I never took my eyes off God. I had to keep praying; when I didn't feel like praying, I had to pray some more. And then when I fell down, I had to have faith that my God would be right there to left me up. I had to keep watching my savior, because I knew that he had something in store that was greater than me. So, no matter where you are, pick yourselves up, dust yourselves off, and keep your eyes on the prize, Jesus. As is stated in Psalms 121:1-8,

I will lift up mine eyes unto the hills, from whence cometh my help. My help cometh from the Lord, which made heaven and earth. He will not suffer thy foot to be moved: he that keepeth thee will not slumber. Behold, he that kee-peth Israel shall neither slumber nor sleep. The Lord is thy keeper: The Lord is thy shade upon thy right hand. The sun shall not smite thee by day, nor the moon by night. The Lord shall preserve thee from all evil: he shall preserve thee from all evil: he shall preserve thy soul. The Lord shall pre-serve thy going and thy coming in from this time forth, and even for evermore.

He has got something unimaginable in store for you. What are you waiting for? Please, wait on the Lord, because during your waiting period, he is sculpt-ing a magnificent, new, and wonderful you. Molding and cutting off all the bad and ugly things you have picked up along the way. He is making you good from the inside outward; this is where the true magic is for everyone. A person looks inward at the soul for a mate. It won't take our God long, for we are his masterpieces, made in his perfection. Pray for your spouses and wait on the Lord! Please, don't become impatient, for this is your trial time. A time when out of your impulsiveness comes mistakes, unforgettable mistakes, sometimes surrendering your life before your time kind of mistakes. As it states in Psalms 27:14, "Wait on the Lord: be of good courage, and he shall strengthen thine heart: wait, I say, on the Lord." If you do this, you will have the one that you could have only dreamed of.

A Prayer for You

Dear heavenly father, I come to you asking for a special blessing upon each of the individuals who have taken the time to read my life story. Let their hearts be filled with confidence and courage so that they will be pushed forward in their lives. Show them unusual favor so that for every closed door, there is an open door that they may walk through it immediately. If there is any illness in their body, they are healed, because you said in Isaiah 53:5 by your stripes we are healed. And Lord, as you walk with them, tell them where to go, when and how they should get to their next assignment. Do not let your children be afraid, for it is said in Isaiah 43:1, "Don't fear for I have redeemed you, I have called you by name; you are Mine." Lord, please don't forget to meet every one of your children's needs, wants, and desires. Father, I just give you all the praise and all the glory, and I declare and decree it right now in Jesus' Mighty, Miracle-working name that it is done. Amen, Amen, and Amen!

I Dreamt of a Man

You see, I dreamt of a man
A man that would love me until the end of time
I dreamt of a man
A man that would love his family more than himself
You see, I dreamt of a man
That would love me like I was unforgettable,
like I was a part of his soul,
like I was someone he could not bear to see hurt or living alone in this world,
like he saw a magnificent painting, and suddenly, he was looking at ME!
You see, I dreamt of a man, but why hasn't a man dreamt of me?

An Apology for my Enemies

To my enemies, I apologize to you for me not staying down in the mud no matter how many times or how hard you kicked me down, I apologize.

To my enemies, I apologize to you, and I am so very sorry for me having a mind filled with nothing but the wisdom of God, that your lies, deceit, and manipulation could not go through the battlefield of my mind and win. But then you rage an attack on me, it was so powerful that I thought, surely, I have lost all sensibility, but I came out with my mind intact, and I said to you, I am so very sorry.

To my enemies, I apologize to you for me not dying when you tried your very best to kill me, but my God said NO, Not Today!

To my enemies, I want to apologize to you, for I am truly sorry for not being shattered and broken when family and friends turned and walked away, but instead, I kept my eyes on Jesus! I am sorry.

To my enemies, I apologize to you for the marriages that you placed me in that failed because of the Jezebel spirits that were meant to destroy me, but instead, they made me stronger and brought me closer to the God that I serve. I do apologize.

Ah, to my enemies, I apologize to you, and say to you that I am truly sorry for everything

But just you remember this, now I am good, so very good
Hahaha, I am GREAT!

Notes

Holy Bible, YouVersion.com. Accessed 2018-2020. KJV
Minister Kevin L.A. Ewing, Witches and Warlocks, pt. 3, YouTube.